THE CENTRAL TEXAS GARDENER

EX LIBRIS

Martha J. Latta

I0963101

The Central Texas Gardener

By
CHERYL HAZELTINE
and
JOAN FILVAROFF

Illustrations by KATE BERGQUIST

TEXAS A&M UNIVERSITY PRESS
College Station and London

Copyright © 1980 by Cheryl Hazeltine and Joan Filvaroff
All rights reserved

Library of Congress Cataloging in Publication Data

Hazeltine, Cheryl, 1942–
    The central Texas gardener.

    Bibliography: p.
    Includes index.
    1. Gardening—Texas. I. Filvaroff, Joan, 1931–
joint author. II. Title.
SB453.2.T4H39   635′.09764   79–28226
ISBN 0–89096–078–X
ISBN 0–89096–086–0 pbk.

Manufactured in the United States of America
THIRD PRINTING

Sharing has made our garden grow.

Contents

List of Illustrations

Preface

> When once fully explored, however, such was the
> tempting beauty of the landscape upon its borders,
> that no dangers could deter the settlers from seek-
> ing an abode in a region, that in appearance, rea-
> lized their most seducing dreams of a paradise upon
> earth.
>
> John M. Niles, *South America and Mexico*
> *with a Complete View of Texas*

WHEN the Filvaroffs first settled in Austin a good while ago, we moved into a house in a lovely area with many trees and older homes. Immediately we were faced with two new and knotty problems: bamboo was taking over the small yard, and an army of unattractive black bugs was trying to take over the house. To learn about these local adversaries, we went to the library.

Here the first seed for this book was sown. The librarian explained there was really only one, none-too-recent book on gardening in this area; she wished it were otherwise. In passing we might mention that an insect book led to an eventual detente with the roaches; however, we moved before we had done an adequate job in uprooting the bamboo.

It was that later move that made the Filvaroffs and the Hazeltines neighbors. Then we discovered that the Hazeltines too had faced gardening challenges and had noted the frustrating lack of published materials.

Throughout the next few years, both authors' perceptions of the need for the book were strengthened, particularly as we learned more about the special environment of this area—its soil and climate—and as we witnessed the growing number of people who were migrating here from many different areas of the country. There was a sense that the right approach might answer a lot of questions and save others from asking, "Why didn't someone tell me?"

The authors combined forces and began to make inquiries. We were encouraged by the county horticulturist, nursery experts, and many friends to pursue our efforts to assemble a gardening manual for the area.

From the beginning, we aimed to provide a basic gardening text that would include procedures and practices the average gardener and homeowner needed to know. We did not intend to present an encyclopedia; rather, we wanted to emphasize general information that would be easy to find, realistic, and practical. To this end, we have included the plant varieties we think are best suited to the climate and other physical conditions of Central Texas. Because common names differ from region to region and can be so numerous for an individual species, we have followed the common names with their scientific names in parentheses. This, we hope, makes it possible to locate plants easily and to have their proper names for identification purposes. Each plant has at least two Latin names: the first, always with its initial letter capitalized, is the genus name. The second name indicates the species, a more narrow classification than genus; its first letter appears in lower case. Where many species of a given genus are appropriate or available, we have used *spp.* (plural of the abbreviation for species) as the inclusive term.

The *Central Texas Gardener* encourages the use of native plantings and those developed especially for this area in landscape design and gardening. It directs the reader to specific sources available from the state's excellent agricultural facilities, from which further information may be obtained.

Additionally, rather than lay down pat rules, we have attempted in this book to stimulate personalized gardening, the urge to experiment, and a love for nature and the process of growth. In the course of this, some of our personal preferences have most certainly surfaced; after you read this book, we hope yours will, too.

The authors wish to give special recogniton to the following, on whose works we have relied for much valuable information: Ted L. Fisher, Travis County Extension Horticulturist, for material on vegetables, trees, and shrubs; Robert A. Vines, *Trees, Shrubs and Woody Vines of the Southwest;* Donald Wyman, *Gardening Encyclopedia,* for material on trees, shrubs, and flowers; and the Texas Agricultural Extension Service for its many publications on vegetables, fruits, flowers, and plant diseases. We appreciate, too, the help and support of Amy Filvaroff, who typed our manuscript, Peggy Dominy, Ellen Filvaroff, David Filvaroff, and Richard Hazeltine.

We are also very grateful for the valuable information we received in conversations with the following people: Marvin L. Baker, Tarrant County Extension Agent; Clinton Benjamin, The Horticultural Center, Austin; Don Freeman, Austin Rose Society; John Griffiths, state climatologist; Cynthia Walters Henderson, Dallas County Extension Horticulturist; the staff at Howard Nursery, Austin; Mike Lancaster, Austin Rose Society; P. J. Louis, U.S. Weather Service; Roy and Deena Mersky, Austin; Joe Montgomery, Austin; Dick and Natalie Palmer, The Gardener, Austin; George Richter, Grounds Maintenance Supervisor, University of Texas at Austin; Murffy Robinson, Murffy's Nursery and Ranch Supply, Round Rock; Luke Thompson, Natural Science Center, Austin; and John Vaught and Mrs. Ethel W. Johnson, Vaught Nursery, Austin.

THE CENTRAL TEXAS GARDENER

The Climate Where We Live

> In the spring I have counted one hundred and thirty-six different kinds of weather inside of twenty-four hours.
>
> Mark Twain, "New England Weather"

Most Central Texans agree that they live in the best part of the country, if not of the world. Ample sunshine, an abundance of greenery, and a great expanse of beautiful skies delight the natives and attract an increasing number of migrants from the north.

One of our friends insists that summer is the only sure season in Texas—sure to be hot; the rest of the year almost anything can happen. Another popular saying here is, "If you don't like the weather, just stick around for twenty-four hours." Both sayings speak to the great and sudden shifts in weather, particularly in winter when northers—cold winds out of the north—appear, often dropping the temperatures fifty degrees Fahrenheit in a matter of hours. While all of Central Texas shares this fickleness of weather, there are noticeable variations in the general climate from north to south and from east to west, even in this relatively limited area. Within our subtropical region, Dallas and Fort Worth are more apt to have a taste of snow in the winter, or worse yet, of the ice that comes when it's too cold for rain. The northern part of our region is also likely to be somewhat cooler in the summer.

From May through September warm, humid, tropical air swept in from the Gulf of Mexico by prevailing south-southeasterly winds dominates the Texas weather scene. Moving across the hot land, the warm air gives rise to those glorious cumulus clouds so characteristic of the Texas summer sky. This same tropical air mass which is responsible for our thundershowers and an occasional hail storm prevents air pollutants from accumulating in Central Texas.

These climatic conditions strongly affect gardening in Central Texas. To be more precise, which plants grow and how well they grow and produce is determined largely by three major climatic factors: temperature, water supply, and light (length of day and intensity). Two of these factors, temperature and light, are beyond the control of the backyard gardener, and her or his success will increase with the acknowledgment of that fact and the attempt to work in harmony with the realities. These elements are interrelated and so variable—especially in Texas—that gardening is a different experience each season. Perhaps that is why we always have something to say about the weather.

Temperature

Central Texas' climate is really dominated by two features: the prolonged high temperatures of summer and the sudden shifts of temperature in winter. Temperatures in our region top the ninety-degree mark between 87 and 116 days annually, whereas there are only 24 to 44 days in winter when the mercury drops to thirty-two degrees or below. But those ninety-degree days tell only a partial story. Many warm areas of the country at least see their temperatures fall significantly at night (e.g., Wichita, Kansas; Albuquerque, New Mexico; Sacramento, California), giving plants much relief from the blistering heat. In Central Texas, though, minimum daily temperatures for July and August rarely dip below seventy-three degrees.

High average temperatures and the frequent abrupt changes we have in our weather influence our plant selection and care. Because cold fronts often arrive overnight, depart, and arrive again just as suddenly, plants may not have time to provide their own natural defenses. If they fail to go fully dormant or if they bloom prematurely, for example, a quick hard freeze can kill them. Even evergreens are more likely to be damaged by a sudden drop in temperature than by a slower drop, which would give them time to acclimatize. Nonetheless, unless a freeze is unusually long, hard, or sudden, even bulb plants such as ranunculus and anemone, which may appear before their prescribed time, will survive nicely in the mild Central Texas winter.

Although Central Texas is best suited to semihardy and subtropical plants, we are constantly tempted by occasional minor successes and attractive offerings at the nursery to try our hands at varieties better adapted to other temperature zones. Gardeners in San Antonio may be fooled into thinking that they can consistently grow bananas after one or two atypical harvests, while Dallasites may eschew wise advice to regard tulips as annuals if several successive cold seasons result in successful blossoms. And in Austin, ever-hopeful residents frequently try for the best of all possible worlds, planting species from the tropical, semihardy, and hardy categories. Some years it works, but don't count on favorable results over the long term.

While it is true that gardeners cannot change the temperature at will, there are a number of measures that will moderate its effects and improve chances of success for those plants that grow only marginally in our climate. First, because site selection can mean the difference between survival or doom for such plants, it is important to give careful consideration to the sheltering effects of buildings, fences, hedges, and plant groupings.

The threat of unusually early or late frosts on vegetables, less-than-hardy shrubs, or houseplants that have been sojourning out-of-doors often can be diminished by a hosing down or, if possible, by setting out the sprinkler for the duration of the freezing period. As water freezes, it gives off heat, which in turn warms the air surrounding the plants. It is important to remember that plants that have suffered light frost damage should be allowed to warm up slowly and naturally. Watering after the frost would only mean another sudden change in the temperature, which could be more detrimental than a light frost.

Protective coverings made of cloth or paper can insulate tender species during these hazardous times. Avoid using black plastic in such instances, though; its direct contact with plants will only increase frost damage.

But don't be discouraged by these seemingly painstaking measures. They all may be obviated by carefully selecting from the many wonderful varieties of trees, shrubs, flowers, and vegetables that flourish without such special attention in Central Texas. We recommend that the tender exotics be planted in pots for patio use

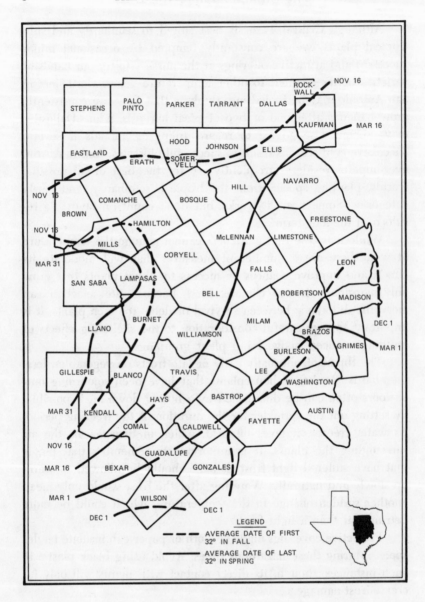

Figure 1. First and Last Freeze Dates

during the growing season and brought inside to winter in a cool and light location.

While an important consideration for all plants, temperature becomes a more significant concern for the vegetable garden. Temperature defines the growing season, which lasts generally from the last to the first freeze (see figure 1 for first and last freeze dates in Central Texas). Not all plants, however, do equally well through the whole growing season. For each species there is a minimum, optimum, and maximum growth temperature. The optimum temperature will vary according to the growth stage of the plant—that is, seedlings have lower optimum temperatures than the same plants at a more mature stage. So we see that temperature affects not only which plants are ideally suited for a region but also when they should be planted. Information about optimal temperatures is seldom available to the average gardener, and certainly it is not our intention to burden you with statistics and jargon. It is, however, helpful when you are selecting varieties, particularly vegetable varieties, to understand that these differences in temperature tolerances are why some vegetables are classified as cool-season crops and others are warm-season crops. Those that are cool-season crops put on their best growth while temperatures are moderate—spring and fall. Warm-season plants will do best when planted so that peak summer temperatures occur during their growth stage. In Central Texas, generally high summer temperatures over an extended period favor planting warm-season crops. Cool-season crops must be planted more judiciously.

Since Central Texas covers a large region, with variation in altitude and proximity to the Gulf coast and substantial differences in distance from the equator, there are important variations in the growing season for areas even within this region. Figure 2 sketches three zones within Central Texas based on the average length of the warm season.

The growing season in this part of Texas is long. At the northern boundary, Dallas–Forth Worth, the season lasts 240 days, with the average first frost occurring about November 12, and the last frost on March 17. Austin has a 260-day season, with the first frost expected near November 22 and the last frost about March 7. In

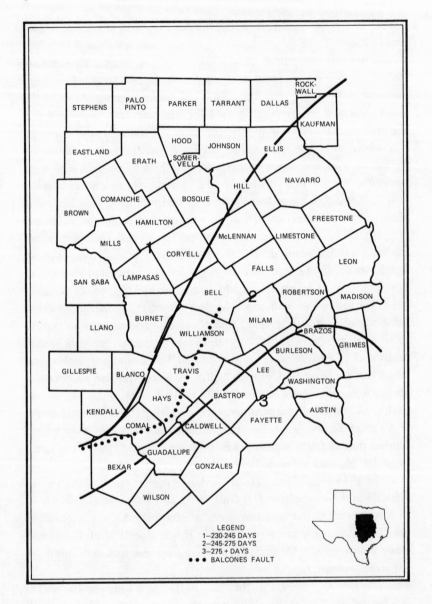

Figure 2.   Average Length of the Warm Season

Waco, first frost comes about November 18, and the average last freeze date is March 16. In San Antonio, the average first freeze comes around November 26, and the last about March 3, giving that area an average frost-free period of 268 days. This extended growing period which our area enjoys means that vegetable gardeners get a chance to put in two crops a year. For planting dates see "A Vegetable Primer," chapter 12.

Light

Light affects the growth and the food and seed production of plants. As there are warm-season and cool-season plants, there are also short-day and long-day plants, that is, plants that need more or fewer hours of sun each day. Goldenrod, hibiscus, and spinach are examples of long-day plants; salvia, asters, and chrysanthemums prefer shorter periods of daylight. Asparagus, narcissus, and foxglove are not especially sensitive to the length of day. Our suburban fall garden, surrounded by tall trees, always fades as the days grow shorter and the light from a lower sun is blocked by the house and trees.

While the gardener cannot add hours to the day or subtract them, she or he can use siting to influence the amount of sun plants receive. Plants recommended for full sun in many gardening books and on seed-packet instructions often can do well in partial shade, particularly in mid-afternoon, in Central Texas.

Water

Many of the ornamental plants and vegetables we want to grow would not survive our climate if we were not able to affect their water supply. Heat, periods of low humidity, and wind increase the rates of evaporation and transpiration (the process by which water and carbon dioxide are exchanged through cells in the leaves of plants), leaving the plants with a deficit of moisture. Plants growing in soils with little capacity to hold water (especially sandy soils) will need watering more frequently than those in better soils. This is another reason why the gardener must pay attention to where she or he sites the plants, in order to assure convenient watering. It may even be a good idea to consider installing an underground watering system before beginning a lawn and basic landscaping (see chapter 4).

Rainfall in Texas is just as erratic as the sudden changes in winter temperature that we discussed previously. Not only is the rain unevenly distributed through the state; the amount may vary tremendously from year to year. The Hill Country is one section that sees more years of below-average rainfall than above-average. Generally in Texas, precipitation increases as one goes from west to east. The average annual precipitation range for our section of the state is 27 to 36 inches. April, May, and June are our wettest months, with September often spilling rains from dissipating tropical storms. Winter precipitation usually comes in the forms of drizzle, light rains, and fog. In other seasons, violent thunderstorms, occasionally accompanied by hail, are common. On September 9 and 10, 1921, for example, Thrall, Texas, experienced the worst rainstorm ever recorded in the continental United States, when 38.2 inches of rain fell in a twenty-four-hour period.

Current theories hold that torrential rains occur when warm, moist air masses from the Gulf of Mexico collide with drier, cooler air from the north and west.[1] These heavy cloudbursts occur more frequently along the Balcones (Spanish for *balconies*) Escarpment, a geological fault zone that lies roughly parallel to Interstate Highway 35 from San Antonio to Waco. Formed about 40 million years ago, when rock strata fractured, the fault's numerous limestone springs have long provided the water to attract human settlement. Indians camped along the fault line long before the white man entered Texas.

Topographical features also determine how runoff from heavy rainfalls is dissipated. Where natural drainage channnels are gently sloped and valleys are flat and broad, runoff is relatively slow. This situation is more typical east of the Balcones Fault. In the Hill

[1]*Austin American-Statesman*, November 9, 1976. Victor R. Baker, of the Department of Geological Sciences at the University of Texas at Austin, is quoted on this by the newspaper.

Country, where the soil is shallow and the slopes steep, runoff tends to be rapid and consequently lost in flooding.

Weather in Central Texas is nothing if not capricious. One strategically timed frost, hailstorm, tornado, heat spell, or whatever can bring an entire vegetable season to a halt and do severe damage to trees and landscape plants. The wise gardener therefore considers climate both in the original selection of plants and in the care she or he takes to make the plants, especially nonnatives, prosper.

Soil and Its Conditioning
The Raw Materials

Our soil belongs also to unborn generations.
Sam Rayburn, "On Conversation"

SOIL—a miraculous mixture of minerals, air, water, and organic matter; as old as the ages, ever changing, continuously renewed. How well it performs depends on its texture, structure, and chemistry. Ideally, it is composed of 45 percent inorganic minerals, 5 percent organic matter, and 50 percent pore space shared equally by air and water. The solid-matter particles should be balanced in size to permit good drainage, adequate aeration, and thus proper nutrient intake by vegetation. Soil of this quality rarely occurs in nature; most soil is, instead, a mix of three basic types.

Soil Types

Clay is composed of minute, tightly arranged particles. When wet, it becomes sticky and plastic. Water drains slowly; erosion and runoff become serious problems. Water replaces air in the pore space and slows the release of nutrients to the plants. During the dry season, clay hardens and cracks, upsetting root systems and hastening evaporation. Easily compacted, it is referred to as heavy soil.

Sand particles are very large, as much as twenty-five times larger than clay particles. Sand drains too rapidly, causing nutrients to leach away before they can be used by the plants.

Loam, a mixture of large and smaller particles, provides moderate drainage and good aeration. It is good for fast and deep root development and nutrient retention. Because well-drained soils tend to harbor fewer diseases, loam is a healthy soil.

Of the ten distinct vegetational designations of Texas, four converge on Central Texas, each with its own well-defined soil characteristics (see figure 3).[1] The eastern counties occupy the regions identified as the Blackland Prairies and the Post Oak Savannah. The fertile prairies are extensively cultivated. The Blackland Prairie soils are largely calcareous (containing calcium) clay, although there are large sections of acid, sandy loams. The Savannah soils are acid and generally loamy. Some sections of the rolling north-central Cross Timbers contain a large portion of rock fragments. There the sandy to clay loams are neutral or slightly acid. The soils of the Edwards Plateau, or Hill Country, are mainly clay on top of limestone. They range from fairly deep in the eastern section to very shallow with a good percentage of rock fragments in areas west of the Balcones Escarpment.

How difficult your soil is to improve depends on the kind of soil it is, its depth, and the number of rock fragments you have to remove. For example, clay soils' seemingly overwhelming problems of poor drainage, inadequate aeration, and limited nutrient retention can be corrected by spading or rototilling in sand, gypsum, and organic matter (peat moss, compost, or manure). The sand and gypsum will help to create air spaces and to lighten the soil. Organic matter benefits the soil by holding the fine clay particles together in large "crumbs" and by releasing nutrients as the matter decays. This decomposition takes place rapidly at first, then slows considerably as the organic material becomes humus (an advanced state of decomposed organic matter). Since humus will eventually break down into elements, organic matter must be added repeatedly to maintain good soil structure.

If you live in the Hill Country, you may also hit caliche—the impervious upper crust of calcium carbonate that forms on the stony soil of arid regions—after digging only two to four inches. The depth of the caliche may vary from several inches to several feet. If it's too deep, you may want to plant in another location or in a raised bed. Shallow caliche can be broken up with a pick and discarded.

[1]Frank W. Gould, *Texas Plants: A Checklist and Ecological Summary*, MP-585/Revised (College Station: Texas Agricultural Experiment Station, 1975).

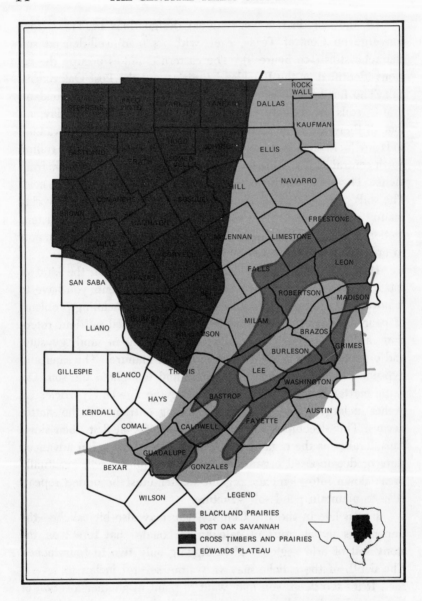

Figure 3.   Soils of Central Texas

Having come to terms with rocks and caliche, you are ready
to attack the clay. First, dig the soil to about one spade's depth,
eight or nine inches, if possible. Spread sand or gypsum to a depth
of two inches and organic matter to a depth of four inches, and
incorporate them. If you are using a spade or fork, mix the additives by inserting the tool at an angle and turning it from side to
side, rather than by inverting the soil. This turning method gives
an even distribution by allowing the new material to filter down.
Your labors will be well rewarded if you are able to prevent the
formation of hardpan, an impervious layer of soil particles so
tightly packed together that drainage is impossible. A deadly condition for plants, hardpan is a serious problem for clay soils that
receive heavy foot traffic, particularly in wet seasons.

Should you live in one of the few pockets of sandy soil that
our region contains, you can improve your soil's ability to retain
moisture and nutrients by adding two to three inches of compost
or peat moss and working it well into the soil.

If these chores sound arduous, don't despair. Few gardening
joys compare with that of turning heavy clay into friable soil—
that is, soil that crumbles easily when damp. It will remain a
source of pride whatever the season, and the effort it requires deep-
ens the satisfaction.

There is always the alternative of buying garden soil, but beware of bargains; good soil is expensive. Make sure what gets de-
livered to your yard is what you ordered. Ask your dealer about its
origin and whether it is weed free. "Store bought" soil will be
likely to require some conditioning and will certainly benefit from
a healthy dose of organic matter.

The particle composition of soil is not the only characteristic
to affect gardening. Among other factors are the pH level and the
availability of nutrients.

Soil pH

The acidity or alkalinity of soil is measured on a pH scale
from 0 (most acid) to 14 (most alkaline); pH 7 is considered neutral. When the pH is too high or too low, the availability of nu-

trients to the plants is reduced, and the resulting deficiencies lead to poor growth. Although most things will grow in soil with a pH between 4 and 8, most fruits, flowers, and vegetables do best in soil between a pH of 6.5 and 7.0.

In many areas of Central and North Central Texas, the soil is very alkaline, with a pH of 7.5 to 8.5. At these levels iron is unavailable to the plants, and the resulting deficiency, iron chlorosis, is a common problem. Symptoms of iron chlorosis are easy to identify: yellowing leaves with their veins outlined in green. Liquid iron, applied as a leaf spray, is the quickest remedy for this condition. Copperas, compost, sulfur, iron sulphate, or cottonseed meal should be added to the soil to help reduce its pH.

Excessive acidity can be quickly reduced by adding lime. However, this is not a common problem in this region, and bear in mind that many plants and vegetables grow best in neutral to slightly acid soil.

Soil pH should be checked before you embark on any major planting. Also, find out the pH preference of the plants you wish to grow and decide whether you want the extra trouble of maintaining the proper soil pH (the water in much of this area is also alkaline); if not, substitute something more tolerant of the native soil.

Plant Nutrients

Plants require sixteen nutrients; the three primary nutrients, which are needed in the greatest quantities, are nitrogen (N), phosphorus (P), and potassium (K).

Nitrogen stimulates growth and the production of plant protein and gives plants rich green color. It is especially important for leafy vegetables and large-leafed plants. However, it is an element that quickly gets leached away. Plants that suffer from nitrogen deficiency may yellow, and their older leaves may drop. Stunted growth, delay in bud opening, smaller leaves, fewer flowers, and smaller fruit may also result from a lack of nitrogen.

On the other hand, beware of the consequences of nitrogen oversupply: too-rapid growth that results in spindly, weak stems, too much leaf growth, and plants that bloom too late in the season.

Phosphorus stimulates vigorous growth of seedlings, the production of fibrous roots, and seed production; it is important for better plant use of soil moisture and the production of plant sugars. Plants that are deficient in phosphorus display symptoms similar to those of nitrogen deficiency. However, the leaves of phosphorus-deficient plants are usually dull green, tinged with purple. Often the entire plant is dwarfed. There is little danger of excess phosphorus.

Potassium's role in plant nutrition is less easily defined than that of nitrogen and phosphorus. It is believed to contribute to normal cell growth through cell division and to act as a catalyst in the formation of proteins, fat, and carbohydrates. Plants are heavy users of potassium, and a lack of it results in leaves that turn ashen and have curled tips and edges.

Calcium, magnesium, and **sulfur** are secondary nutrients, which are generally supplied by the soil. The seven remaining nutrients—iron, zinc, manganese, boron, molybdenum, copper, and chlorium—are trace elements. In our alkaline soils, iron and manganese are present but frequently inaccessible to the plants, as previously mentioned in the soil pH section.

Soil-testing kits are available, ranging in price from two to twenty-five dollars. These kits measure soil pH and indicate the amounts of nitrogen, phosphorus, and potassium your soil needs. Accuracy may be hard to achieve, as it depends on the tester's ability to match the colors of the tested soil to a color chart. We think your best bet is to take advantage of the comprehensive soil-testing service available through your county agricultural extension agent and performed at Texas A&M University.[2] For a nominal fee, your soil is tested for nitrogen, phosphorous, and potassium, for trace elements, and for pH. Recommendations for soil improvement will be made according to the land's intended use: lawn, vegetables, and so forth.

---

[2]For soil analysis, send soil samples to: Soil Testing Laboratory, Texas Agricultural Extension Service, College Station, Texas 77843. Special mailers are available at your county agricultural agent's office.

Fertilizer

Even a casual reading of the gardening literature quickly reveals a plethora of recommendations for fertilizing. The confusion this causes is only compounded when your nurseryman doesn't carry the particular formula you ask for but offers a substitute that you are not sure is comparable. Then there is always the old-timer who swears that her or his magical concoction works wonders for every living thing or the organic gardener who insists on only organic fertilizers. Confronted with a blur of fact and lore, most of us who garden for pleasure are left completely frustrated.

Generally, 5–10–5 is a good formula for a balanced fertilizer. The numbers refer to the percentage of nutrients contained in the fertilizer mixture. Since the numbers always are given in the same order—nitrogen (N), phosphorous (P), and potassium (K)—a one-hundred-pound bag of 5–10–5 would contain five pounds of nitrogen, ten pounds of phosphorous, and five pounds of potassium. While 5–10–5 is an excellent balanced fertilizer for many garden needs, certain circumstances require special mixes, which will be noted in the text.

While fertilizer applications should be made according to the kind, age, and special needs of the plant(s), the guidelines for 5–10–5 fertilizer offer a good general picture and a basis for comparison.

Flower beds	3–5 lbs. per 100 sq. ft.
Bulbs	1–3 lbs. per 100 sq. ft.
Vegetables	3–5 lbs. per 100 sq. ft.
Evergreen shrubs	3–6 lbs. per 100 sq. ft.
Evergreen trees	2 lbs. per inch diameter of tree at chest height
Deciduous ornamental trees	2–4 lbs. per inch diameter of tree at chest height

Ideally, soil should be moist and foliage dry when fertilizer is applied. Always water thoroughly after fertilizing.

ORGANIC VS. INORGANIC FERTILIZERS

Before petrochemicals were introduced to agriculture and gardening, farmers and gardeners met their crops' and plants' nutrient needs with manure, cottonseed meal, bone meal, and blood meal. While many gardeners today insist that these organic sources are preferable to inorganics, such as superphosphate, iron chelate, and ammonium sulfate, it is very difficult to find experimental evidence of differences in plants produced by organic or inorganic nutrients. Releasing their nutrients more slowly, organics are longer lasting than chemical fertilizers. They are also more expensive. But using natural products has a strong and undeniable appeal—from both aesthetic and conservation standpoints. Because the home gardener gardens on a small scale, she or he is in the enviable position of being able to make a choice.

Recently, foliar feeding has gained popularity. This method involves mixing water-soluble chemicals with a prescribed amount of water and applying it directly to the entire plant with a watering can or sprayer. Because leaves absorb most efficiently in the morning, it is best to apply the foliar fertilizer at that time of day. Be sure to wet both sides of the foliage thoroughly. To be most effective, this method of feeding flowers, vegetables, shrubs, and small trees should be practiced every ten days to two weeks from the first feeding in early spring to the end of September, when most growth (fall vegetable and flower gardens being the exceptions) begins to slow.

Compost

Mix a pile of damp leaves, grass clippings, and some vegetable wastes from the kitchen, and within a year you can be harvesting a crop of "black gold." We have already discussed the importance of organic matter to soil structure and chemistry. Compost is the least expensive and most readily available source of organic matter.

Making a compost pile is a pleasure that compares to that of improving soil structure. Its appeal is easily understood, for it involves the ultimate recycling and can be practiced on a very simple level. Composting is a living process—the decomposition of organic matter by microorganisms—and an understanding of what goes on inside that heap of vegetative wastes can prevent you from coming up with just a pile of soggy leaves at the end of the year.

Two types of bacteria—aerobic, which live in the presence of air, and anaerobic, which live in a wet, airless environment—set to work to decompose organic matter. Anaerobic bacteria tend to smell bad and work more slowly; they are responsible for many people's fears about a compost pile. Fortunately, they can be replaced by the aerobic variety by keeping the pile moist, but not soggy, and by turning the compost to introduce oxygen. Constructing a compost bin from chicken wire or with boards spaced so as to allow air circulation will keep the pile exposed to the air. Many people place a stick in the middle of a compost pile to provide air to its center.

A bin or a container of some sort (roughly five feet square and five feet high) is necessary to prevent leaves, grass, etc., from scattering and to allow sufficient heat buildup. Heat is generated by the multiplying organisms; its presence indicates that the compost pile is functioning. The optimum temperature range for a compost pile is 104 degrees to 140 degrees. Around 158 degrees the pile will suffer "thermal kill" and will cool to somewhere within the optimal range. It is a delight on a frosty morning to see the steam rise when you wiggle that aerating stick in the middle of the bin and know that everything is going just fine.

Moisture is another necessary factor in the environment of the bacteria. A healthy compost pile will be between 40 and 60 percent moisture, or as damp as a squeezed sponge. Below 40 percent, the rate of decomposition will decline; above 60 percent you risk having anaerobic bacteria, with their accompanying odors, take over.

Carbon and nitrogen present in the organic matter provide the fuel and building materials for the growth of the bacteria. The proper proportions of these two elements—expressed as the carbon-nitrogen or C/N ratio—are essential to the success of the compost. Too little nitrogen will result in failure of the compost to heat up and a slow rate of decomposition. The optimal ratio is in the range of twenty-six to thirty-five parts carbon for each part nitrogen.

Because the C/N ratio is the most important aspect of composting, we provide a list of carbonaceous and nitrogenous materials in table form.

C (carbonaceous)	N (nitrogenous)
leaves	weeds (do not use those which have
hay, straw	gone to seed)
sawdust	plant residues from garden
wood chips	grass clippings
chopped cornstalks	vegetable kitchen waste

You can see from the list that nitrogenous materials tend to be green, succulent, or leafy in comparison with the woody, drier carbonaceous materials. If the compost seems to be working too slowly, you can add a little nitrogen in the form of fertilizer.

Grinding the organic materials (particularly cornstalks and the woody parts of plants) is helpful but not necessary. It speeds the decomposition process. A variety of textures provides for air circulation and prevents compaction. Finished compost has a dark, rich color, an earthy odor, and a fluffy structure. Often the origin of the materials can still be identified.

Odor has rarely been a problem in our compost pile. When it has, turning has been sufficient to eliminate the offending anaerobic bacteria. You will want to avoid using animal products—waste or meat scraps. They tend to create odors and attract pets and vermin. Flies occasionally buzz about in summer. Some people cover the pile with a plastic sheet or tarpaulin to control this problem, but this tactic reduces air circulation. We have found that keeping vegetable kitchen wastes covered with grass clippings is an adequate solution. From time to time, we do see crawly insects in the outermost layers of the pile, but they never appear in the finished product. By carefully selecting the location of your compost pile, you can eliminate the minor irritants and be free to enjoy this earthy delight.

The method outlined at the beginning of this section will yield ripe compost in a year or less. More detailed and considerably more laborious recipes have been devised to provide compost in a few months or in even as short a time as two weeks. But the home gardener is seldom in such a hurry. All composting methods are based on the requirements discussed above, which should be repeated:

1. C/N ratio
2. moisture
3. aeration
4. sufficient size for heat retention

Chemical analyses show nitrogen levels of compost to be between 1 and 3 percent and phosphorous and potassium levels under 1 percent. For this reason, compost should never be considered a substitute for fertilizer. Instead, it should be used as a soil conditioner, in which capacity it functions invaluably to increase water-holding capacity, provide nutrients for soil microorganisms, and improve soil texture. Compost is most effective when used with organic or chemical fertilizers.

3

Plant Propagation
Getting Something Started

And for all this, nature is never spent;
There lives the dearest freshness deep down things. . . .
Gerard Manley Hopkins, "God's Grandeur"

NOT only is propagating one's own plants more rewarding and economical than buying everything already started at the nursery, sometimes it is the only way to acquire certain varieties. This is particularly true for many desirable native species that are overlooked by the large, out-of-state, commercial growers who supply many of the local garden centers. We found that even at the better nurseries, which either grew their own stock or relied on local suppliers, the variety of native plants was limited.

Basic propagation methods discussed here are seed planting, layering, cuttings, and division.

Seeds

While most flower and vegetable seed packets include excellent instructions for outdoor planting, a few words of caution are warranted. A moist but not soggy garden is best for seed sowing. Many novices have a tendency to plant their seeds too deeply, which may result in seeds' failing to germinate. If you follow the packet directions for spacing, you will have plenty of seed, perhaps even enough to share with a friend.

Starting seeds in flats is a time-honored practice among serious gardeners. It is an excellent method for planting very fine or expensive seed or seed that requires a long time to germinate. A number of growing media are suitable for starting seeds in flats, which are shallow boxes that have holes or cracks provided for drainage. Some gardeners like to mix up a combination of equal parts sand, compost and peat, and garden loam. Others prefer to use a sterile medium such as vermiculite to prevent damping-off, a soil-borne disease that commonly attacks seedlings. Whatever you use, it should hold water well and be fine enough to permit the tiny seedlings to grow unencumbered. Make certain the medium is distributed evenly throughout the flat. Pat it firmly with a block of wood. Next, water it and allow it to drain.

Some gardeners prefer to treat their seeds with a fungicide before planting. This is easily done by placing a small amount of fungicide in the seed packet and shaking it vigorously, giving the seeds a light coating. Recommended fungicides are captan, Semesan, and Spergon.

Very fine seed may be sown over the planting medium, left uncovered, and gently pressed into the mix with a block of wood. Medium-sized seed should be sown in shallow furrows and covered by the amount of seeding mix indicated for such seeds. Drop large seed into holes made by your finger or a pencil and cover to the depth specified in the instructions.

Now you should cover the flat with a couple of sheets of damp newspaper or a pane of glass. Avoid direct sunlight and place in a warm, light spot. You must not allow the planting medium to dry out. Check daily, and water when necessary. When the seeds have germinated, it is time to remove the newspaper or glass pane.

As the plants continue to grow, give them more and more light, always taking care that the medium remains moist. Spraying is an excellent way to deliver water to the fledgling plants. It is important to keep the moisture level constant, avoiding periods of drought and flooding. The optimum temperature for seedlings is about sixty degrees. If too warm, the seedlings will become spindly and may delay putting on their first pair of true leaves (the first leaves to emerge are referred to as seed leaves). When the plants have developed two sets of true leaves, it is time to transplant them to another flat. The soil mixture in this second flat should be slightly richer than the one used in the first. A standard recommendation is one part compost or moistened peat moss and two parts loam.

When transplanting to the second flat, be sure that the holes you make for the plants are deep enough for the seedling root system. Seedlings should be planted two inches apart and transplanted to the garden several weeks later when the leaves of one plant touch those of its neighbor.

Newly transplanted seedlings frequently show signs of shock; the most common sign is wilting. This strain on the young plants can be reduced by transplanting during the late afternoon or early evening. If you must transplant during midday, be sure to provide some shade for the seedlings. Always gently firm the newly transplanted plants.

If your garden plans don't call for a large number of vegetables or flowers, starting seeds in peat pots is highly recommended. Although it is a bit more expensive, the ease of transplanting with this method makes it well worth the extra pennies. When the plants are ready to be planted in the garden, simply plant the entire pot; you thereby greatly reduce the risk of root shock.

Layering

The two methods of layering, ground and air, are old and reliable ways to propagate. Ground layering, the easier but slower of the two, is achieved by securing a lower branch of the plant you wish to duplicate in a shallow depression in the soil with a hook of wire, plastic, or wood. The terminal end of the branch is left free to produce new growth. The root-forming process may be speeded up by making a small cut in the underside of the branch where it will contact the soil. When the branch is firmly rooted, it may be severed from the mother plant and transplanted to another site.

While many plants set roots in this manner in one season, favorites such as camellias, azaleas, and hollies may take two years before their roots are developed sufficiently to be severed from the main plant. The best time for separating the two plants is in the spring.

For plants whose erect growth habit precludes ground layering, air layering is a good alternative (see next figure). After re-

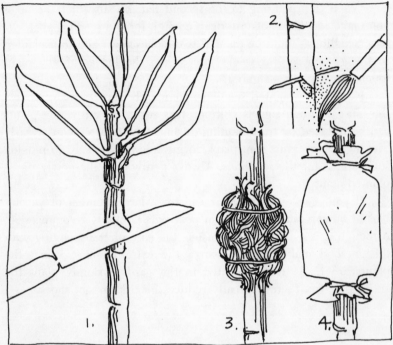

PROPER AIR-LAYERING PROCEDURE

moving the leaves on a six- to eight-inch span of a branch, make
a notch with a sharp knife about twelve to eighteen inches from
the terminal end of the branch. Moisten the cut with water, and
dust lightly with a rooting hormone. Next, apply enough moist
sphagnum moss to provide a three- to four-inch cover to the wound
and top with plastic. Be sure to secure both ends of the plastic
firmly with rubber bands or tape to prevent evaporation. Check
periodically to see that the moss is always damp. Add a small
amount of water if necessary. When a healthy set of roots has developed, it is time to remove the new plant and give it a place of
its own. Late spring and early summer are the best times to do air
layering. The root-making process should be complete by September, giving the new plants ample time to get a good foothold in
the soil before the frost.

Cuttings

Stem cutting is another successful method of propagating plants you discover away from home. Softwood cuttings (those taken from plants whose stems are green and flexible) are best taken in late spring or early summer. If you take the necessary precautions to prevent the cuttings from drying out, you should have very little trouble producing healthy plants in three to six weeks.

Cut a five- to six-inch terminal stem just below a leaf node and remove all but the top two leaves, which will continue to produce food. Moisten the bottom end and dip one-half inch of the stem in a rooting hormone. Shake off the excess hormone powder. Make a hole with a stick in a damp rooting medium such as vermiculite or coarse sand, and insert the stem. Be careful not to allow the rooting hormone to rub off the stem. Keep the medium moist. Because the cutting is still producing food, it will need light, but not harsh, direct sun that will dry it out. The cutting can be covered with polyethylene film to keep in moisture, although frequent misting (spraying) may be sufficient. It will not damage the cutting if you lift it out occasionally to check whether the rooting process has begun. The cutting is ready to be transplanted to a permanent location when the roots are one-fourth to one-half inch long.

Hardwood cuttings are taken after the season's growth has become wood, usually in late winter or early spring. Using leafless sections six to ten inches long, cut off the tip about one-half inch above a leaf node. Then at the lower end, make a diagonal cut (to distinguish top from bottom) just under a leaf node and dust with a rooting hormone. Place the cutting at least two to three inches into a moist rooting medium and leave the top exposed to the air. Roots should form within three to five weeks. Again, do not allow the rooting medium to dry out.

Division

In addition to multiplying your plant and flower stock, division—the easiest propagation method—revitalizes plants that lack vigorous growth and are producing smaller flowers than they should be. It is an ideal procedure for perennials.

Spring-flowering plants may be divided after flowering, usually in the early summer. Early summer bloomers are best divided in early fall, and fall bloomers in the spring. Shallow-rooted plants may be lifted from the soil and gently pulled apart, while those with larger root systems may need to be pried apart by working two garden forks back to back. Discard old or damaged roots and dust the newly divided sections with an all-purpose fungicide before replanting. It is a good idea to work in a small amount of 0–20–20 fertilizer at this time. After replanting, cut back the stems by one-half to restore root-leaf balance, and water thoroughly.

Some plants that are divided easily are asters, daisies, day lilies, chrysanthemums, irises, and violets. True bulb plants, like daffodils, should be dug up after their foliage has withered and dried. Remove the small bulblets from the mother bulb and replant. Plants with tuberous roots, such as dahlias, are divided by cutting the parent into sections. Each new section must contain an eye or undeveloped bud. Dust the new sections with a fungicide and allow to dry for several hours before storing.

Bearded iris and other plants that grow from rhizomes (underground stems) should be cut into sections with a sharp knife that has been dusted with a fungicide. Replant only those outer sections which contain new plant growth. Corms, the solid underground stems of plants like crocus and gladiolus, may be cut into halves or thirds, each new section containing part of the center of the parent corm. Sometimes corms will develop another large corm or several smaller cormlets, which may be separated from the parent and replanted. The infant cormlets will require two to three years to develop.

Selection of Plants
and Landscaping

> To own a bit of ground, to scratch it with a hoe, to
> plant seeds, and watch the renewal of life—this is
> the commonest delight of the race, the most satisfac-
> tory thing a man can do.
> Charles Dudley Warner, "My Summer in a Garden"

THIS is the "do as we say, not as we do" section. Which means
that impulse buying of plants admired in nurseries is not recommended unless you want to start a nursery of your own.

Today many people live on small lots—a quarter-acre or less—
and we've observed a tendency to overplant rather than under-
plant. For those new homeowners who do not want to hire a landscape architect, here are a few basic suggestions that should prove
useful.

Start by becoming familiar with the stock in your local nurseries. Be sure to have paper and pen along so that you can note
the most attractive shrubs and trees and their important characteristics and needs—evergreen or deciduous, size, sun or shade, flowers, etc. Right here we want to put in a big plug for native plants;
they are well adapted to the climate and soil, usually require less
care, and look "right" in the landscape. Having said all that, we
hasten to add that some slow-growing natives, such as mountain
laurel and live oak trees, are on the costly side.

We suggest you make a simple drawing of your lot and house,
shading in areas to show natural features, including plants in exis-
tence, the slope of the lot, and man-made additions, such as sidewalks and driveways (see the example on page 30). Be sure to put
in compass points on your drawing so you'll know from what direction the sun is shining.

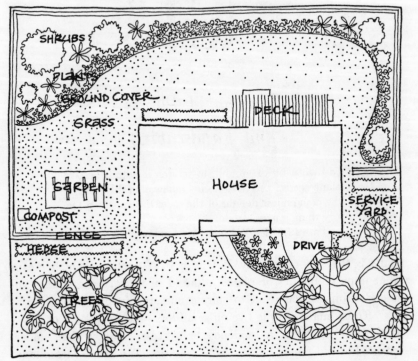

A LANDSCAPE PLAN

As you sketch, you will become aware of the individuality of your lot—its basic shape and special areas of interest, such as a trio of native yaupons in the backyard or a distinctive live oak in front. To get a good, balanced view of what the landscape needs, try looking at your lot from the street or from a neighbor's house and then look out at it from your own house and from different vantage points on your lot.

Study the shape of your lot and of your garden space. While a long, narrow garden may be somewhat limiting, it also offers the opportunity for special long-distance effects. It may be easier to work with a level lot, but a sloping one might include striking terraces or an impressive entrance with attractive broad steps.

Now that you are armed with a list, a sketch, and a great incentive to create, you can begin your do-it-yourself plan. The first decision is whether to have a formal garden, where plants placed on one side are duplicated on the other side for a symmetrical, rather severe look, or to opt for an informal garden, where there is no precise system of balance but rather a unified variety of plant material. A third choice, which is particularly well suited to less-developed neighborhoods and larger lots, is the natural look, where little is done to control or change what nature has provided and dense foliage dominates the setting.

As you make your plan, remember that there is a strong rationale for taking your time in carrying out a landscaping design, although some ambitious people want to run right out and buy everything at once. Selecting the basics, then living with them while sorting out the other possibilities has, we think, much to recommend it. In this way you can become more aware of new plants and seasonal plants and how they will fit into your garden.

As you proceed, keep in mind the basic landscape areas to be addressed: the public area, the private area, and the service area.

The public area is primarily the front yard and that area in public view. Your immediate neighbors see it all the time; it is also open to inspection by passersby. Your plan for the public area should be simple, in good taste, and in harmony with the neighborhood, of which it is an integral part.

Certainly there is room for individual expression in the front yard—for instance, a raised bed or a striking hedge—but either should complement the entire view and not strike a discordant note. A short time ago, we heard about a man who lived on a well-trafficked corner lot. He decided to put a picket fence all around the front and side yards and painted the fence bright green, so that it dominated the view for several blocks. The fence is no longer, and we were told that the neighbors' objections had hastened its removal. In this case, the desire for privacy might have been fulfilled less obtrusively and more attractively with shrubs for screening purposes. Actually, the homeowner wound up using a nice border of ligustrum bushes.

The private area is usually the backyard. In our congenial climate, it is often the recreation center for barbecues, swimming, and general relaxation. This is a good spot for a flower or vegetable garden and the specimen plants and statuary that you had to have but that wouldn't look right in front.

Many homes nowadays are located on small lots and are contemporary in architectural style. Often such a home is placed near the front of the lot, so there is ample private area but very little public area. Another result is the proliferation of backyard cedar fences, which, along with certain shrubs, provide the desired privacy for the area.

The service area is often on the side of the house, where air conditioning compressors, pool pumps, alleyways between houses, and compost piles are found. Here the plants chosen would most likely serve practical, protective, and screening functions. For one tea-drinking friend, the area between the garden hose and the air conditioner proved to be the perfect spot to turn loose a bed of mint.

After you've decided whether to go formal or informal, you can choose what kind of lawn you want and how extensive it should be (see chapter 5). Remember to think about ground covers and other alternatives to lawns (see chapter 6), which can complement plants and provide cover where other plants won't grow. While you are thinking about lawns, you should decide whether or not to include an automatic sprinkler system. Their biggest disadvantage, in our opinion, is economic—they are costly. Of course, if you are very ambitious and handy to boot, you might try installing your own system. Just remember, this should be done before the lawn is put in.

Next, using your sketch, find the focal point in the front yard. This is usually a doorway, but it could be a picture window. Arrange your plantings to emphasize this feature. Above all, don't overplant—keep your plan simple. It's easier to add than to subtract plants. Also remember that growth characteristics of plants should be considered: height, rate of growth, and general appearance while developing. As you make selections, you may want to choose plants that mature at different rates; if you choose all slow growers your yard will look underdeveloped longer than you'd like.

Borders of broad-leaved evergreen shrubs (see chapter 9) have traditionally been selected to soften the line of the foundation, especially in the front of the house. Additionally, such shrubs provide heat and cold insulation and help prevent soil shifts or drying, which may cause foundation cracks. If you choose to follow this tradition, be sure to select species that will be the proper height when mature (generally low to medium in front of one-story homes) and will be easily maintained. Ligustrum, pittosporum, and boxwood are some of the more popular candidates.

For visual and textural interest, be sure to include some flowering shrubs (see chapter 9). Despite the extra care they require, you will be amply rewarded every year at blossoming time by azaleas, crape myrtle, and camellias, to name just a few possibilities. Flowering evergreens, such as gardenias or azaleas, may be used in front of the foundation; deciduous flowering shrubs, such as flowering quince and plumbago, look better year-round with taller evergreens between them and the foundation. Generally it gives a more unified appearance to think in terms of small groups of plants rather than one of this and one of that, which can look fragmented.

When considering trees (see chapter 8), think of their major functions: framing, shade, windbreak, accent, and background. Trees also provide oxygen to the environment, filter the air, and help reduce sound pollution. Wildlife is attracted to trees and shrubs with edible fruit and nuts. One word of caution: do not choose a tree simply because it's a rapid grower; consider all attributes when making your selections.

Of course you mustn't forget the flowers for gardens, borders, and bouquets (see chapter 11). There are so many to choose from; we suggest you try different kinds in your flower garden every year. They are such a pleasure outside and—those you cut—inside, too. If used near the foundation or property boundaries, flowers look better with a background of evergreen shrubs.

Remember that vines (see chapter 10) can be very useful in covering unattractive areas or on fences and walls. And, of course, that sturdy favorite English ivy also winds attractively around tree trunks.

Many homeowners will find room for a vegetable garden on their lot (see chapter 12). There is no substitute for the pleasure of bringing in a sweet head of lettuce or a pot of crisp beans to add to the supper table. For the same reason, there is also a good deal of interest in growing fruit and nut trees.

A few other tips may help prevent common mistakes. Don't

plant too close to the house, driveway, or sidewalk. Large trees, such as oaks and elms, should be planted at least twenty feet from the house, so their branches don't overhang the structure and their leaves don't clutter the eaves. We are reminded of the friend whose control is tested every year when her husband uses the hose to wash the leaves out of the eaves of the second-story roof, making the most dreadful mess of the first-floor windows.

Shrubs should be far enough away so that when they mature they won't touch the walls. Do not plant tall trees under utility wires or poplars and willows where their aggressive roots might damage underground drainage pipes.

To leave enough space between shrubs, use the figure for the height and spread of the plant as a general guideline. In other words, leave a six-foot space between two azaleas that will reach six feet eventually.

To give them their proper due, use specimen or unusual plants sparingly, particularly in the front yard. If you are infatuated with a recent discovery (newcomers are particularly prone to this weakness), we suggest you go home and find a proper spot for the plant before buying it. This is a good way to eliminate the I-have-it, where-should-I-put-it syndrome, and it may save you money, too.

One of the bonuses of being a gardener is sharing your enthusiasm and successes; just for being visible in the garden you may be offered some lovely plants from your neighbors and friends (as well as some good gardening tips). We once complimented a perfect stranger on a bed of shrubs, and she immediately offered to dig up samples for us to take home. We also have a begonia cutting that came from a six-year-old plant that's produced cuttings for more people than can be recalled.

Once you have decided which plants you want, you may have some difficulty finding them. Although some people have success ordering from well-known national nurseries, we suggest making the rounds locally first. And you do have to make the rounds, because the stock on hand, professional assistance, and prices asked vary greatly according to the nursery and the time of year. The weekend newspaper ads often offer the best means of monitoring prices and shipments of new plants. When you're doing the actual buying, keep the following suggestions in mind.

It's a good idea to buy young plants, at about half the size they'll eventually reach. While it is natural to opt for a good-sized tree, a smaller one (six to eight feet) is easier to plant and more apt to survive.

Look for healthy plants with new growth, blemish-free leaves, and an abundance of buds. Stay away from plants with shriveled bark, too many dead twigs, or brown or yellow-green leaves. Check leaves for discolored spots, which may mean fungus disease, or holes, which indicate the presence of insects. Remember that a soft, white, cottony substance means mealy bugs are present. To check for mites you can place a piece of white paper under the leaves and shake the plant; if tiny moving dots appear on the paper, it's a bad sign.

Many plants in nurseries today are sold in the containers in which they are grown. However, there are some that are grown in fields, dug up, and put into cans shortly before they are sold. These generally are less desirable because they may have lost a number of roots when they were dug up. If the roots stick out above the soil and the sides of the can, the plant has recently been moved. You may also ask the nurseryman to lift the shrub out of the container. You should see many roots tightly packed on the outside of the soil ball; if you don't or if the soil ball is loose and crumbly, the shrub may not have been in the container very long. When buying bare-root plants, make sure the roots have been wrapped in damp material to keep them from drying out.

While making your rounds of the nurseries, keep an eye out for special fibrous containers that dissolve when put into the soil. These are often used for roses, especially. They have the obvious advantage of lessening transplant shock and keeping good soil around the plant. In clay areas you need to cut through the bottom of the container to make sure the roots can get out soon enough.

As you read on through the following chapters, remember: in landscaping you can't overvalue planning and forethought. Correcting mistakes by moving trees and shrubs is possible, but it certainly isn't much fun.

Lawns
Planting and Keeping Them

I believe a leaf of grass is no less than the journey-
work of the stars.

Walt Whitman, "Song of Myself"

A good lawn wins praise from more than the poets; it is the subject of admiration to all who see it. Without doubt it is the most
important feature in planning the area surrounding the home.
Besides being aesthetically and emotionally satisfying, it has important functions, such as preventing soil erosion, muffling noise,
reducing glare, contributing oxygen to the environment, filtering
harmful pollutants from the air, and providing an inexpensive rec-
reational surface.

Of the hundreds of species of grass that grow in Texas, only
a few are suitable as turf grasses. The three most commonly used
in this area are St. Augustine, bermuda grass, and zoysia, all warm-
season turf grasses that grow in the late spring, summer, and early
fall. Ideally, all should be planted in the spring or early summer.[1]

St. Augustine (*Stenotaphrum secundatum*), which was brought
to America from the West Indies, is a broad-leaved perennial with
runners (stolons) on the surface. It grows well in this area and is
also a favorite in coastal locations like St. Augustine, Florida, from
which it derives its name. Either sod blocks or runners (strips of
sod) are planted to start the lawn. Don't ask for seed when you buy
St. Augustine, or you may be given carpet grass, which, although
similar, is actually field grass and not suitable for lawns in this

---

[1]By the way, according to professionals in the laundry business, the best
way to remove grass stains from colored fabrics is with denatured or rubbing
alcohol. Place the spot in the fabric on a clean rag or a paper towel and press
it firmly with your fingers. You may have to repeat the process several times,
moving the fabric to a clean spot on the rag each time. On white fabrics, use
detergent and household bleach.

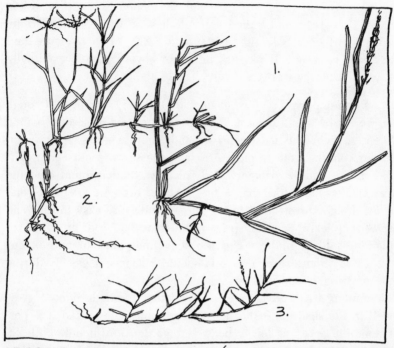

GRASSES: ST. AUGUSTINE GRASS (Stenotaphrum secundatum) 2. BERMUDA GRASS (Cynodon dactylon) 3. ZOYSIA (Zoysia japonica)

area. St. Augustine should be mowed at a height of two to three inches.

St. Augustine is favored for its dense, thick turf which crowds out many weeds and other grasses. It's easy to start and gives rapid coverage. It takes about six months for complete coverage if you use runners or sod blocks cut into small squares and set a foot apart. St. Augustine stays green longer than bermuda grass and grows in either sun or shade.

On the debit side, we find that St. Augustine is susceptible to diseases such as brown patch, St. Augustine Decline (SAD), and leaf spot. It is attacked by chinch bugs and white grubs, is more susceptible to iron chlorosis (iron deficiency), and, according to some experts, needs more water than bermuda grass. In addition, its coarse texture is unappealing to some people.

A new variety of St. Augustine developed by North Carolina State University and called Raleigh has been recommended by several turf experts for its resistance to SAD, its finer texture, and its shade tolerance. If plugged into your lawn, it should eventually take over and be worth the only slightly higher cost.

Bermuda grass (*Cynodon dactylon*) is very popular, although in the Austin area, at least, it apparently comes in second behind St. Augustine. This narrow-leaved and vigorous grass was brought to our country from tropical Africa in the seventeenth century. It has stolons (surface runners) and rhizomes (underground creeping stems). Bermuda grass has a fine texture, drought tolerance, and generally good resistance to turf diseases. It's also easy to start and spreads quickly. Seed or sprigs (small pieces of sod) are used for planting, although the sprigs are sometimes hard to find in our area. For a dense turf, bermuda should be mowed weekly during the growing season at 1 to 1½ inches.

Among its disadvantages, we find that bermuda doesn't grow well in the shade and that its underground stems make it a persistent nuisance in flower beds and gardens. Although both St. Augustine and bermuda grass tend to "brown out" in winter after a frost, bermuda begins to look bad much earlier than St. Augustine.

Common bermuda grass is the most practical and economical variety; the hybrids such as Tifgreen and Tifdwarf give a denser, weed-resistant turf when mowed close and frequently, but they are somewhat more expensive to maintain.

Zoysia grass (*Zoysia japonica*) is a native of Asia and was formerly known as Korean or Japanese lawn grass. With proper care, zoysia makes an attractive turf that resists invasion by weeds and other grasses, as well as damage from insects and disease. It is started with sprigs or sod blocks.

Zoysia doesn't do well in dense shade and is less drought tolerant than common bermuda grass. A slow-growing grass, it may take from one to two years to get the same coverage from zoysia that bermuda or St. Augustine would give in three to six months. For this reason zoysia is not a pest in gardens. However, it turns brown with a frost and stays straw-colored all winter; it's also relatively expensive. In our climate zoysia should be watered frequently and thoroughly and mowed as often as bermuda at 1 to 1½ inches, preferably with a reel-type lawn mower. Both the Emerald and Meyer varieties of zoysia are popular in this area.

Starting a New Lawn

Just when you're most involved with the business of moving, you may be faced with the chore of putting in a new lawn. Sometimes the builder has accepted that responsibility; even then, however, some supervision by the homeowner at planting time may prevent problems from developing later on.

If your home is located in a newly developed, rocky area, the builder will probably have to bring in topsoil. Whether or not topsoil is imported, you should be certain that building debris—stones, lumber, trash—has been removed first and that the area has been properly graded to provide surface drainage. The ground should slope gradually away from the house, walks, and drives.

Once the ground is properly prepared for planting, you may want to make a soil test or send a soil sample to the Soil Testing Laboratory in College Station for analysis (see chapter 2). Some people merely add a well-balanced fertilizer by rototilling or raking it well into the soil. Be sure the lawn area is smooth and flush with walks and drives to prevent mowing and runoff problems.

Although lawns may be started almost any time after the last freeze, in March through September, some installers prefer fall because they avoid intense summer heat. However, you should be sure to allow six weeks of growth before frost time, when the soil gets cold. If you choose spring to start a lawn, the grass will benefit from a longer growing season, but you must be sure to provide ample water and to protect it against the invasion of too many weeds.

If you are using grass seed, buy a quality product with a high percentage of germination and purity. A reputable seed dealer can help you make the best possible selection. We talked to one who said that 90 percent germination or higher listed on the package is a good buy. We suggest using a small seed distributor, but if you prefer hand sowing divide the seed in half. Walk back and forth in one direction sowing the first half; then walk at right angles to the first seeding to sow the second half.

Sprigs, runners, or sod blocks are used to plant St. Augustine, zoysia, and sometimes bermuda. We got good coverage with St. Augustine the first season by planting long runners in rows about ten to twelve inches apart. Remember to select good, healthy sprigs that are not yellowed and that are free of weeds.

After the grass is planted, it should be watered lightly and frequently to keep the surface moist. If you have sown seed, it will take two to three weeks before sprouts appear. As the seedlings develop or the sprigs begin to grow, you should reduce the frequency of watering and increase the amount of water applied at one time. This allows a deep root system to develop.

A new lawn should be mowed when the grass is about 1½ to 2 inches high; St. Augustine should be about 3 inches. Never remove as much as half the growth at one time. Don't be discouraged by weeds; they're bound to pop up at first. We spent time pulling out a lot of Johnson grass the first summer; happily most of it and much of the clover were not around the second year. Frequent mowing, adequate fertilization, and watering all helped. Once a lawn has been established, it still demands this kind of regular care to keep it healthy and attractive.

The three key elements in grass nutrition are nitrogen, which promotes vegetative growth and deep green color, phosphorous, which helps develop a good root system, and potassium, which encourages plant stability, cell strength, and winter hardiness. According to our able county horticulturist, an effective complete fertilizer would have a ratio of 10–10–5: 10 percent nitrogen, 10 percent phosphorous, and 5 percent potassium (or potash). An average lawn needs three to four pounds of nitrogen per 1,000 square feet. A word of warning: too much nitrogen may cause thatch accumulation and greater disease susceptibility.

Many experts recommend water-insoluble fertilizers with their slow release of nitrogen rather than inorganic or water-soluble types. Slow-release nitrogen sources developed especially for turf, such as those with ureaformaldehyde, are sometimes preferred because they last longer and require less frequent fertilization, although they do cost more. Whichever type you choose requires knowing the number of square feet (length times width) of your lot before you make a purchase. The average lot in our area is about 60 feet by 125 feet, or 7,500 square feet.

Most of our neighbors don't fertilize more than once or twice a year; those who expect more from their lawns may fertilize as much as four times annually. For example, one expert told us he gives his lawn a complete fertilizer in February and September and uses a nitrogen fertilizer such as ammonium sulphate in May and July. He also recommends a separate dose of iron for our soil.

On the other hand, a friend with a fine St. Augustine lawn uses only an annual application of a water-insoluble fertilizer with high nitrogen content. A turf grass specialist from the Agricultural Extension Service at Texas A&M University says that an annual fall application in this instance might be adequate for St. Augustine but not for bermuda grass, which requires more fertilizer. Incidentally, a local physicist told us that lightning makes nitrogen available in rainfall—one reason why our lawns look great after a series of electric storms.

Watch carefully, and you can tell when a lawn needs water. It will turn a dark olive color, and the leaves will begin to wilt and curl. Now is the time for a thorough watering, and the emphasis is on thorough. Because of the soil texture, a slow, steady delivery is recommended. We found it necessary to keep the sprinkler in one spot for at least an hour, but the best method is to test the soil for water drainage. Deep watering, about once a week in dry seasons, encourages the development of a deep root system. The best watering time is early in the day; avoid evening watering, as this encourages fungus growth.

Close and frequent mowing of turf grasses is recommended. Unfortunately, some people wait too long to do the job; since the leaves manufacture food needed by the plant, it is damaging to remove one-half or more of the growth at one time. Use a sharp mower that cuts the tips without bruising the plant.

There is some difference of opinion about whether or not to

collect the grass clippings. If you leave them, they do add nourishment to the soil, and if you mow frequently there probably won't be a problem. However, too much accumulation is unattractive and may cause thatch (the spongy turf that collects between the soil and green leaves); for these reasons some people prefer to collect the clippings. If thatch becomes more than three-quarters of an inch thick, it will prevent air, water, and fertilizer from passing through it. This may require the use of a dethatcher, which cuts through the growth and drags it to the surface. These machines may be rented through rental companies. Some garden centers have a chemical preparation for dissolving thatch, but we suggest reading the label carefully. If in doubt, check with your county agent before using such chemicals.

Our type of soil tends to compact, and after a period of time your lawn may require aeration to increase the movement of air and water into the soil and promote deep rooting of the grass. Our county agent said this may be necessary after a period of six years. Some people suggest that a compacted area will be improved by inserting a spading fork deep into the soil, pushing the handle forward and backward, and repeating this every six inches or so. This should work in a small area, but to do the entire lawn you'll want to rent an aerator, which removes soil cores several inches in length. These cores should be broken up afterward or shredded with a mower.

Perhaps you've noticed the neighbors spreading loads of dirt on their lawns in the spring; for some it's an annual ritual. However, this is probably necessary only where runoff creates depressions that need to be filled in.

Proper watering, fertilizing, and mowing are also important for weed control. If that doesn't work, the next step is to hand pull the weeds—no fun, but it helps. Different herbicides are available for specific weeds; it's best to check on what can (and cannot) be used on your lawn with the county agent or a nursery expert.

If you've chosen St. Augustine for your lawn, be on the lookout for trouble from chinch bugs. They're small (one-eighth inch long) and black, with white wings folded over the back; they're particularly active in hot, dry summers. Watch for irregular patches in open, sunny areas of the lawn, especially along a driveway, sidewalk, or the house foundation. The grass turns yellow, then dies and turns brown. You can test for chinch bugs by removing the ends from a tin can, twisting it into the ground near the edge of the damaged area, and filling it with water. If the grass is infested, within five minutes the bugs will float to the top. Diazinon is commonly used to treat chinch bugs and is recommended for the bermuda mite as well. You need a microscope to see the bermuda mite, but if bermuda grass appears stunted and turns brown you should be suspicious and check it out.

Another enemy of Texas lawns is the white grub, the larva of the May or June beetle, which feeds on grass roots. If the sod can be easily picked up, it might be that a number of grubs have severed the plant roots. To check, examine the roots and soil by digging up several sections of sod four inches deep. Treatment with diazinon is indicated if you have more than four grubs per square foot. Watch for grubs beginning in June and throughout the summer.

There are several diseases that threaten lawns in this area, particularly lawns of St. Augustine. Circular yellow or brown patches several feet in diameter (the outside resembles a smoke ring) are symptoms of a fungus called brown patch. This disease is prevalent in the spring and early fall when the temperature is between seventy-five and eighty-five degrees; the fungus stops growing at ninety degrees. A preventive fungicide such as PCNB (Terraclor) or chlorothalonil (Daconil) may be applied beginning in early fall. According to the Texas Agricultural Extension Service (Bulletin L-732), "On lawns where brown patch occurs occasionally, apply fungicide when the disease first appears." Chlorothalonil is sometimes recommended for leaf spot diseases—brown to gray spots which turn into dark blotches on leaves and stems of St. Augustine and bermuda grass, particularly in shaded areas that remain damp for some time.

Just as in humans, a virus disease is the hardest to control in lawns. St. Augustine Decline (SAD) causes mottling of the leaf blade and an overall decline in lawn vigor. Since chemicals won't help, it is suggested that Floratam St. Augustine, which is SAD-resistant, be added to an infected area, where it will eventually replace the ailing grass.

Despite the obstacles to raising a good lawn, there are few greater rewards than a fine expanse of green covering your property. However, there are times when a ground cover other than grass may be desired. This is the subject we will pursue in the next chapter.

Alternatives to Lawns

Pleasures newly found are sweet
When they lie about our feet.
William Wordsworth, "To
the Small Celandine"

A tour of the neighborhood and community will make you aware
of some alternatives to lawns which have eye appeal and which
may also serve special functions. These alternatives include rock
gardens—cacti, succulents, pebble mulches—and a group of ground
covers with many different characteristics.

The term *ground cover* refers to a group of low-growing plants
used in places that otherwise would either have grass or remain
bare. *Low growing* is not a precise term, but for the average-size
home, it would probably mean from three inches to twelve inches
high.

Ground covers vary in several ways. Some are herbs and shrubs
like rosemary; some are vines such as ivy; others are evergreen
plants such as candytuft and liriope; and some, like asparagus fern,
die back in winter.

Unlike grass, ground covers do not do well when walked upon
and therefore should not be used in high-traffic areas. However,
they, along with other lawn substitutes, do have certain advantages
over the standard grass lawn. For one thing, they can be used in
places and under conditions that grass simply cannot. For instance,
some covers, such as lantana and ivy, can tolerate drought, shade,
or more neglect than grass in hot weather. Some other choices
(listed below) prove useful on steep slopes as soil binders, in rocky
areas where the soil is thin, or in areas with poor drainage. A
friend's childhood home included a delightful rock garden, which
followed the curve of an under-the-house driveway. The rock garden

was on an embankment where a lawn could not have been success-fully maintained (the figure shows some good rock-garden plants).

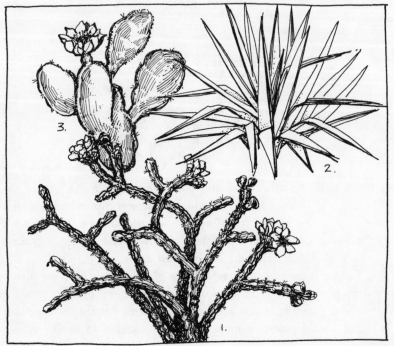

ROCK GARDEN PLANTS: 1. CHOLLA 2. YUCCA 3. PRICKLY PEAR

Additionally, ground covers and other alternatives to lawns have great aesthetic value. There are times when a ground cover adds just the right effect to the landscape. For example, it might break up a large expanse of lawn, relieving the monotony. Or it might make a corner interesting, adding texture and color for all seasons. It might provide an attractive border or accent. A nice ground cover can also provide continuity, blending together unre-lated shrubs and flowers.

In other cases, we have seen decks employed effectively to provide usable and aesthetically appealing areas where homes are built on steep inclines and there are no real backyards, just nature in the raw. Courtyards and patios provide additional options and offer the obvious advantages of year-round places to relax and hold outside get-togethers.

One word of warning: although ground covers and other lawn substitutes may solve certain problems and cut down on maintenance chores, they do not eliminate them. Ground covers require care if they are to thrive, and most of the tasks must be done by hand. Obviously in our hot summers, many (excluding succulents and cacti) require more attention than in other, more moderate climates. Disadvantages of patios include heat reflected from the cement, possible drainage problems during downpours, and maintenance that may include frequent sweeping and hosing down.

Like grass lawns, alternatives to turf require careful planning and preparation if they are to do the job you want them to. Be sure to consider whether you can satisfy the individual requirements of the options you are considering before you make your choice. For instance, succulents require sun, and candytuft needs good drainage.

If you wish to reserve a space for a cactus and succulent garden, be certain to pick a sunny spot and provide for drainage. To discourage those persistent weeds and grasses, try placing a sheet of black plastic over the prepared soil, fastening it with rocks, wires, or stakes, then cutting holes in it to insert the plants, and covering it with pebble mulch. By the way, another effective use of pebble mulches is as borders for driveways and pathways.

Planting a ground cover requires preparation similar to that for planting grass. First, the ground must be properly graded. This is the time to install or have installed a sprinkler system if you are so inclined. Then organic matter, such as manure, compost, or peat moss, can be added to improve the soil. Next, you should broadcast a ground cover fertilizer with nitrogen, phosphorous, and potassium in the ratio of 5–10–10. Spread the fertilizer over the soil at the rate of twenty to forty pounds per 1,000 square feet. The fertilizer and the peat moss should be worked into the soil.

Using the measurements given in the plant list at the end of this chapter, properly space the plants and set them into holes so that the plants are slightly below ground level and will be in a position to catch water. On a slope, it's a good idea to stagger the rows to prevent washouts. Then the area should be mulched with, for example, wood chips or finely ground bark. This procedure helps the plants retain the moisture critical for their survival; the stolons and runners of many ground covers need moisture to root. Mulching also keeps the weeds out and makes the area more attractive. The final step is to water thoroughly.

When you plant ground covers, spacing is important, since you want coverage as soon as possible. Notice in the plant list that small plants, such as ajuga, may be spaced six to eight inches apart, while candytuft needs to be twelve to eighteen inches apart and the larger cotoneasters (see chapter 9) need to be three to four feet apart. The U.S. Department of Agriculture provided the following chart, which shows the approximate area that 100 plants will cover when set at various distances. For example, if you set ajuga six inches apart, 100 plants will cover twenty-five square feet. Closer planting will cover the ground more rapidly but may make your cost prohibitive.

Planting Distance (inches)	Area Covered (square feet)
4	11
6	25
8	44
10	70
12	100
18	225
24	400
36	900
48	1,000

Once the ground cover is established, it requires fertilizing, weeding, watering, and, as indicated above, mulching. Fertilize the plants in autumn and once more in early spring. Water regularly and thoroughly in spring, summer, and fall and occasionally in winter when it's dry. The Department of Agriculture suggests watering whenever the soil is dry to the touch and the tips of the plant wilt slightly at midday. Be sure to prune away dead wood and keep the plants in their boundaries. As we said above, you will need to keep the area free of weeds and stray grass.

A list of popular ground covers follows, including a separate list of herbs that are suitable for use as ground covers. Choose the one whose characteristics best suit your needs. Ground covers include some vines and low shrubs, which are discussed in separate chapters. They are listed here, with a cross reference, to emphasize their potental uses as ground covers.

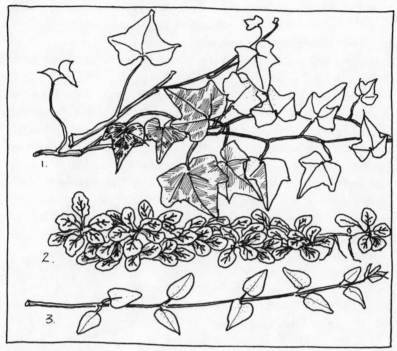

GROUND COVERS: 1. ENGLISH IVY 2. AJUGA 3. VINCA MINOR

Popular Ground Covers

Ajuga, also called **Carpet Bugle** (*A. reptans*). One of the more striking ground covers, ajuga has green, purple, or variegated evergreen foliage, which turns a reddish bronze in fall; it has clusters of small blue flowers in spring. The plants should be set six to eight inches apart in spring. They will multiply rapidly by sending out stolons; the new plants can be divided from the parent plant after the new spring growth. Ajuga likes rich, moist soil, does well in the shade, and is subject to nematodes and fungus.

Asparagus Fern (*A. sprengeri*). A favorite for hanging baskets, the asparagus fern also softens the landscape in select locations, which have a good supply of sun. It is a light, delicate green, and in spring clusters of pinkish white flowers appear, which in turn give way to minute red berries. The soil should be enriched with organic matter; this fern grows best when fertilized several times a year and watered frequently. Propagate by seed and root division. The plants should be set fifteen to eighteen inches apart; be sure they have plenty of room or you will have to watch out for entanglements with other shrubs. Prune in early spring to six to eight inches in height.

Candytuft, Evergreen (*Iberis sempervirens*). This flowering evergreen is often seen growing in six- to twelve-inch-high mounds in rock gardens. It has dark green foliage and round, attractive clusters of tiny white flowers, which appear in spring and which make it an attractive border plant for walks or taller plants. Candytuft prefers enriched, well-drained soil and full sun. It is easily started from seed; if you start it from plants, space them from twelve to eighteen inches apart. Plants can be propagated by cuttings or division after the flowering. For a neat appearance and more vigorous growth, shear plants back after they bloom.

Cotoneaster. *See shrubs, chapter 9*

Creeping Myrtle. *See Periwinkle, Common*

Euonymus. *See Wintercreeper*

Fern. *See Asparagus Fern*

Honeysuckle. *See vines, chapter 10*

Ivy. *See vines, chapter 10*

Jasmine. *See vines, chapter 10*

Jessamine. *See vines, chapter 10*

Lantana. *See shrubs, chapter 9*

Lily Turf, also called **Mondo Grass** (*Ophiopogon japonicus*). Only six inches high, lily turf nonetheless grows densely in grasslike mounds that make it especially useful under trees or as a border plant. It likes organically enriched moist soil, and it does well in full sun to partial shade. A dark green all year long, in early summer it has small lavender flowers followed by clusters of blue berries. The plants should be set six to twelve inches apart since they spread rapidly.

Liriope (*L. muscari* or *L. spicata*). An evergreen, grasslike perennial that grows up to a foot tall and forms a dense covering for the ground, liriope produces small white or purple flowers on spikes in summer. Similar to lily turf, only hardier and thus a better choice farther north, it makes a fine border plant and ground cover under trees. It tolerates heat and drought and does well in almost any soil and in semishade. Liriope is available in a most attractive variegated form. Space plants about twelve inches apart.

Mondo Grass. *See Lily Turf*

Periwinkle, Big *(Vinca major)*. This southern European native is very much at home in our hot, dry climate. It has glossy, dark green or variegated white and green foliage and funnel-shaped purple flowers in early summer. Plant twelve to eighteen inches apart, preferably in light shade and enriched, moist soil. Once established, it requires little care and will grow to a height of two feet.

Periwinkle, Common, also called **Creeping Myrtle** *(Vinca minor)*. An excellent and popular evergreen ground cover that grows up to eight inches but prefers light shade, *vinca* needs little care. It has dark, lustrous leaves about two inches long and flowers in lavender or white (*Alba* variety). Hardier than *vinca major*, it is one of our best ground covers. Plant in the spring or early fall, twelve to eighteen inches apart. The plants may be divided or cuttings taken at any time. Its trailing growth habit makes it a fine selection for use around trees or on slopes.

Phlox, also called **Ground Pink** *(P. subulata)*. Magenta, white, pink, or violet blossoms one-half to one inch in size cover these rock-garden plants in the spring. The evergreen foliage has narrow, sharply shaped leaves about a half-inch long. These plants seldom grow over six inches tall but often spread several feet. Plant in the spring, in well-drained soil, twelve to eighteen inches apart. New plants are started from cuttings after the plants have blossomed.

Santolina, *See Shrubs, chapter 9*

Sedum, also called **Stonecrop** *(Sedum* spp.). Sedum includes a large group of low, succulent plants that do well in poor soil in rocky places, including rock gardens, ledges, and crevices. Many have evergreen or semi-evergreen leaves, which differ in size, shape, and color. The flowers may be white, yellow, pink, or purple; they bloom, depending on the species, from early spring through the fall. Plants should be set about ten inches apart. Take cuttings or divide old plants to start new ones.

Wintercreeper, also called **Euonymus** (*E. fortunei*). This evergreen vine forms a dense carpet of oval-shaped, serrated leaves that turn an attractive purplish red color in fall. It rarely grows more than six inches tall, and, although it prefers sun, it will tolerate partial shade. Euonymus should be planted at about twelve-inch intervals. It is a good choice for erosion control in rocky areas, especially if you enrich the soil with organic matter. Euonymus tends to be susceptible to scale and powdery mildew.

Herbs as Ground Covers

Sweet-smelling, diverse in texture, adaptable, and often delicately blooming, herbs should not be overlooked as a special category of ground covers. Fresh herbs, so superior to their dried counterparts, are useful in the kitchen, and herbs are seldom bothered with insect problems. These fast-growing plants are very successful where their undemanding requirements of loamy soil enriched with organic matter, good drainage, and lots of sunshine are met. Cutting corners on any of these requirements is bound to bring disappointment. Because we are treating herbs as ground covers here, we will include only the perennial herbs that are suitable to our area.

Chives (*Allium schoenoprasum*). The narrow, tender, reedlike leaves of less than one foot in height make this herb ideal for borders in sunny locations. Readily available at nurseries and supermarkets, small clumps of chives should be planted eight to twelve inches apart. Within a couple of years, you will be able to start new plantings by dividing the groups in spring. To preserve the appearance of the plants, when harvesting clip several whole leaves rather than shearing the plant across the top, as the leaves will turn brown at the cut edge.

Marjoram, Wild, also called **Oregano** (*Origanum vulgare*). Popularly associated with Mediterranean dishes, oregano is easily started from seed planted after the soil has warmed, or it can be purchased in pots from nurseries. Plants should be spaced six to eight inches apart. Growing to a height of one to two feet, the herb has a good tendency to spread.

Mint (*Mentha* spp.). Indestructible and difficult to contain, the mints require plenty of space of their own if they are not to take over areas intended for other living things. Slow and troublesome to start by seed, mint is easily established from root cuttings. Most nurseries carry potted plants of spearmint (*M. spicata*) and peppermint (*M. piperita*) in the spring. Field mint (*M. arvensis*), a North American native and a perennial herb, is often found wild in moist areas. Growing to a height of one to two feet, mint is most attractive when kept clipped somewhat lower. It becomes straggly if permitted to flower. Mint loves moisture and will spread rapidly by underground runners under optimum conditions. It is one of the few shade-tolerant herbs.

ROSEMARY (Rosmarinus officinalis)

Rosemary (*Rosmarinus officinalis*). Dark green, needlelike foliage, a pungent fragrance, delicate, light blue flowers, and an attractive growth habit make this herb, which grows in the form of a shrub, extremely desirable in a rock garden or as a patio border. While it can be started from seed, it is best planted from specimens started at the nursery. It withstands heavy trimming, or its branches can be encouraged to root by being pegged to the soil. Although semihardy, it can suffer frost damage.

Sage (*Salvia officinalis*). A small shrub with pale green leaves and long spikes of lavender flowers in spring, the sage is a hardy herb with a pleasing countenance. Growing well from seed, plants should stand ten to sixteen inches apart.

Savory, Winter (*Satureia montana*). The leaves of the winter savory are stronger in flavor than those of the annual summer savories and enhance hearty stews, stuffings, and meat loaves. A small, evergreen shrub, the winter savory must never be planted where there is a possibility it will stand in water.

Thyme (*Thymus vulgaris*). Delicate, woody stems covered by minute, fragrant leaves form a rapidly spreading lacework mat over the ground. Tiny lavender flowers appear in spring. Thyme seeds germinate quickly. New plants can also be started by stem cuttings, and the robust plants should be set one foot apart.

Tree and Shrub Planting
and Maintenance

Now 'tis the spring and weeds are shallow-rooted;
Suffer them now, and they'll o'ergrow the garden.
Shakespeare, *II Henry VI*

MANY of us enjoy shopping in nurseries and selecting trees and shrubs. The not-so-attractive tasks of planting and maintenance may get less attention, which is unfortunate. Proper planting will get the tree or shrub off to a good start. Winter, when trees are dormant, is the best time for planting; it gives the root system a chance to get established and ready for the big growing season in spring. Bare-root trees are more often planted before the last frost in March. In our climate you can plant most shrubs any time of the year they are available, although your job will be more difficult in the midst of a hot spell. If you plant then, for best results be certain to water very slowly after planting.

First, dig a hole about twice as wide as the root ball and, if possible, one and a half times as deep. If the plant is in a container, the can or pot must be removed by cutting the sides from the top to the bottom. Metal cans should be snipped by the nurserymen at the time of purchase. If the plant is balled and burlapped, do not disturb the wrappings.

Before moving the plant, decide which angle is best and how you wish to position it. If the plant has bare roots, center it in the hole and spread the roots out in a natural manner. Center your balled and burlapped plants; be sure they are standing straight (see figure on page 56). Be sure to plant the tree at the level it was planted in the nursery or even a little lower in the ground (the discolored ring near the base of the trunk indicates the original soil line). Start filling in with topsoil mixed with peat.

Firm the soil with your feet to eliminate air pockets. When the

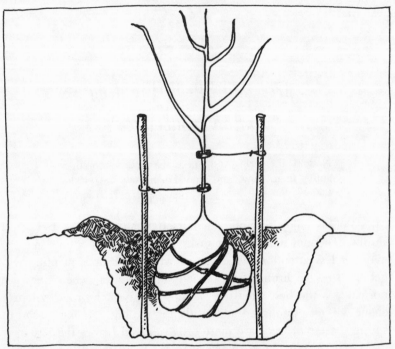

PROPER PLANTING OF A BALLED TREE

hole is about two-thirds full, finish filling it with water. After the water has soaked in, untie the burlap covering and pull it gently away from the top of the soil ball. You can spread it out a bit and leave it to disintegrate in the soil. Finish filling in the hole with soil and peat moss.

Transplanting trees and shrubs from one location to another requires special care. Chances for survival are best if the plant is moved at the proper time—late winter or early spring, just before the growing period begins, or in the fall. Avoid transplanting during the summer months at all costs. During this season the rate of transpiration (the exchange of moisture and gases) is high, and many plants will not survive the shock suffered if they are moved.

The smaller the plant, the easier it is to remove from its original site without major damage to its root structure. The moving of trees with a trunk diameter of two inches or more should be left to experts. Not only do these professionals possess the skills, but they also have the necessary heavy-duty equipment that few of us keep in the garage or toolshed.

When moving the tree, remember that its root system roughly parallels its branches, and that digging should begin outside the drip line. Try to take as much soil with the roots as possible.

Because there is always some root loss in the transplanting process, it is necessary to the plant's recovery to prune the branches to bring both systems back into balance. It is recommended that as much as one-third of the lateral growth be removed. As drastic as this practice seems, plants cared for as directed will recover much more rapidly and will suffer little dying off of limbs.

Transplanting should be completed as soon as possible; roots must not be allowed to dry out. If the tree cannot be replanted immediately, take steps such as covering the roots with wet peat moss to prevent loss of moisture.

Trees like pecans that have long taproots are especially difficult to transplant, and you should attempt to move them only if it is necessary and the tree is small. Even then, transplanting should be done only after the tree has been root pruned at least a year in advance to encourage the development of a strong lateral-root network. Sudden severing of the tap root and transplanting the tree to a new location is almost always fatal.

To give a newly planted tree adequate support to see it through heavy weather, stake the tree to two six-foot poles with guying wires. Be sure to insert the wire through segments of garden hose where it touches the tree to prevent it from cutting into the tree.

Build a ridge of soil three to six inches high around the edges of the hole to form a watering saucer and fill it with water. An application of root-stimulator—a moderate-phosphorus, low-nitrogen fertilizer—is often recommended at this time to overcome "root shock" and to get the tree off to a good start. If you use good soil for backfill, no other fertilizing will be necessary for the first year. Remember, if there's no rain, fill the saucer with water several times a week for the next few weeks. After the initial period, it helps to fill the depression with an organic mulch of peat moss or bark chips to preserve moisture and discourage weeds. Some experts suggest keeping the newly planted trunk wrapped for six months from the ground up to the first branches to help prevent sunburn or scald, which can crack the bark.

Keeping the root zone of a fruit tree evenly moist for its first year is important for a good start. Remembering that the tree's root system parallels roughly its branch system, water slowly from the branch line inward. A soaker hose works well here. Keep the saucer you formed at the time of planting hoed to prevent the soil from cracking and to discourage invasive weeds and grass, or mulch the saucer to a depth of two to three inches. Fruit production of mature trees will be more abundant and of better quality if the trees can be spared the devastation of severe drought. Watering deeply is the important point to remember.

Follow the same basic planting procedure for shrubs as for trees, omitting the step calling for guying wires. Use all peat moss as a planting medium for azaleas and half peat moss, half sandy loam for camellias, gardenias, and other acid-loving plants.

Fertilizing

Fertilizing and pruning are the two basic maintenance procedures for trees and shrubs; both are most important in young plants. If they are done properly early in the plant's life, the plant will grow healthily and attractively with little need for more than occasional assistance from you.

Plants in need of fertilizer will lack terminal growth and have many dead branches, and the leaves will be yellow or a paler-than-normal shade of green. Stunted growth and early loss of leaves also are common symptoms of low fertility. Annual surface applications of a fertilizer with a 2-1-1 ratio, e.g., 12-6-6, distributed evenly under the branch spread in late winter or early spring are adequate to maintain basic good health. Late summer applications may be needed for fall and winter growing periods in areas where the danger of frost is slight.

Outlined below is a standard procedure for fertilizing trees and large shrubs whose needs exceed routine care.

1. Using a crowbar or auger, dig holes from twelve to eighteen

inches deep, if possible, and two feet apart under the drip line (the outer ends of the branches).

2. Measure the tree at chest height (about four feet). For tree trunks less than six inches in diameter, use two to three pounds of fertilizer per inch. Trees larger than six inches in diameter will require three to five pounds per inch.

3. Distribute the fertilizer evenly in the holes.

4. Fill in the holes with a well-aerated mixture of soil, sand, and peat moss. This will make water and air available to the tree.

5. Water deeply.

Severely distressed trees may require liquid fertilizer injections by a professional.

While most of the evergreen ornamentals require less fertilizer than the deciduous plants, maintaining proper soil acidity is a special concern for broadleaved evergreens, such as magnolia and loquat. At the very onset of chlorosis symptoms (yellowing leaves with prominent green veins), these plants should be given applications of iron sulfate or chelated iron. Foliar spraying is the most efficient method of application.

The heavy bloomers—azaleas, camellias, and gardenias—should be fed with an 8-12-4 fertilizer at six-week intervals from April to September. For hints on the special care of roses, see chapter 9.

Pruning

Whether pruning is an art or a science we are not about to decide here, but it does come with its own nomenclature and an arsenal of specialized tools that should impress anyone. Despite its considerable trappings, few people understand pruning or take the principles seriously. To most of us, pruning means the removal of unwanted limbs and branches. Actually, proper pruning rejuvenates older plants, contributes to general plant health, determines the shape of the plant, and affects the number and size of blossoms and fruit.

The most obvious reasons to prune are to remove growth that is interfering with utility lines and other structures and to eliminate wood that is damaged, dead, or diseased. After pruning diseased wood, always wash your tools in a ten-to-one water-chlorox solution before going on to prune healthy branches.

Two basic pruning techniques are **heading** and **thinning**. Heading, or cutting the branches back to the buds, will produce a bushy look and may be just right for controlling a rangy plant, such as a fruitless mulberry. It is, however, a method to be used judiciously, as it can alter the shape of a tree radically. In thinning, one removes entire branches back to the main stem. This technique opens up growing space and encourages a natural line of growth. A clean cut with a minumum stub is the desired end of the pruning cut. This is achieved by holding the cutting edge of the tool adjacent to the part of the plant you wish to retain. The result will be satisfactory in terms of both aesthetics and healing.

Prune at the proper time. What the proper time is varies with the species, but a few basic rules can be stated here. Late winter, when the plant is dormant and its framework is exposed, is the best time to prune deciduous summer- and fall-flowering trees and shrubs. Trees, such as maples, that are inclined to "bleed" heavily when cut should be pruned in late summer or fall, not in late winter or early spring. Spring-flowering plants, since they form their buds the season before they bloom, should be pruned after they have flowered. Evergreens can be pruned in January through March and again in midsummer, leaving the new growth ample time to harden before the first killing frost. Light summer pruning and pinching back of terminal growth is particularly recommended for flowering fruit trees and ornamentals. Done routinely, these steps can make extensive dormant-season pruning unnecessary. Pinch out new shoots that are not desired as branches when they are three to four inches long. This method, repeated every six weeks throughout the growing season, encourages shapely growth. Periodic attention will pay dividends; plants that have been neglected too long can seldom be restored to their best shape.

Do not top trees unless they are diseased. Topping will destroy the natural growth lines of the trees. Prune suckers at the base and watersprouts on branches. Both forms of growth are easily identified. Watersprouts are most common on fruit trees. They shoot straight up and are different in appearance from other branches.

Suckers grow from the roots at the base of the tree or shrub. Both are rapid growers and are visually undesirable.

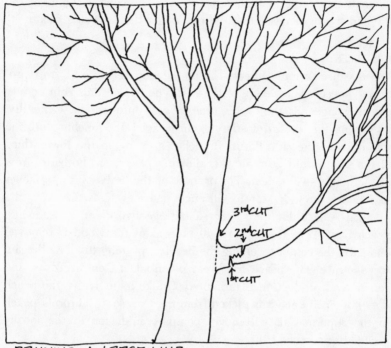

PRUNING A LARGE LIMB

Large limbs should be done in sections or with the aid of a rope for support (see the sketch). A heavy limb may tear before the cut is completed, stripping the bark and increasing the size of the wound. Never twist a pruning tool; twisting, too, will tend to tear at the bark. In most cases, unless you are agile and have a good deal of confidence and the proper tools, it is advisable to hire a professional to prune larger trees. Here the adage "you get what you pay for" is true. Just because a fellow has a pickup and a few tools doesn't mean he knows much about trees. Often, these operators take off far too much leaf area in order to impress the customer that he is indeed getting his money's worth.

CONIFERS

Conifers should be pruned, if at all, after the new growth

has been completed and before it has become woody. The "candles," as the new shoots of pines are called, should be cut at about one-half the length of their new growth. The central candle of the top and the branches should be cut longer than the side shoots.

FRUIT TREES

Because pruning affects the abundance and size of fruit produced, specific knowledge of the tree type is essential. Your county extension agent is the best source of such information. Generally, in pecans the central leader is encouraged by pinching off the soft buds of the side limbs. Branches growing in the lower third of the tree should be removed, allowing permanent limbs to grow at the height of five feet. Tip pruning of the limbs by three inches in January through March will encourage new growth.

Three scaffold limbs form a basic network for a producing peach tree. After three years, 40 percent of the wood is removed annually, the center receiving the heaviest pruning to allow the sun to penetrate. The peach has great potential in Central Texas, and commercial production is promoted. Unlike many fruits, the peach does not ripen once it is picked from the tree, so a California peach in the supermarket will never compare in flavor to the locally grown, tree-ripened fruit.

The pear, with the exception of its susceptibility to fire blight, is the easiest fruit tree to maintain. It requires no pruning or fertilizing—practices which would, in fact, result in excessive, unwanted growth.

SHRUBS

Because shrubs are put to so many different uses, it is difficult to state hard and fast rules for pruning them. While pruning in the correct season is essential for the flowering shrubs, a broader latitude is possible for the evergreens. The larger and fast-growing plants, such as pittosporum, photinia, and ligustrum, should be kept under control by occasional thinning and pinching back throughout the growing season. When buying shrubs, keep in mind your landscape needs and the ultimate size of the plants in question. Many of the best-looking ornamentals—nandina, pittosporum, abelia, several hollies, and yaupon, for example—are available in dwarf form. The dense foliage and compact growing habits of these shrubs make them highly desirable in many landscape situations and reduce pruning chores.

Two commonly observed pruning errors that should be avoided are cutting back winter-killed branches prematurely and tapering shrubs, particularly hedges, at the base. Gardeners, eager to assess damage and to rid the landscape of unsightly blackened branches, often prune plants back to green growth too early. First, the ability of many plants to revive as soon as spring arrives is astonishing and makes such pruning unnecessary. Secondly, early pruning increases the shrubs' vulnerability to possible late frost damage. Wait until all danger of frost is over or until new growth appears before correcting winter's crimes.

For some reason, gardeners love to cut back the frequently sparse or straggly lower branches of shrubs. Unknowingly, they succeed only in compounding the problem they attempt to remedy. Lower limbs must be given adequate air and sunlight if foliage is to be encouraged. The base of a shrub always should be at least as wide as the top. When clipping hedges, taper slightly toward the top of the plant.

So let caution be the byword when pruning or even thinking of pruning. The mistakes one can make here are easily irreparable and even dangerous. Tempering your enthusiasm is difficult on a beautiful spring day, when it feels so good to be outdoors and working in the garden, but do it. It pays. We know from first-hand experience.

Perhaps in Eden perfect fruit fell from the trees in great abundance; however, having been cast out of Paradise, man must work hard for those fruits. Pruning, watering, rigid schedules of spraying and fertilizing are necessary for fruit and nut production and for the flourishing of other trees and shrubs. The abandonment of these practices will result in a rapidly declining yard.

Trees: A Checklist

A man does not plant a tree for himself; he plants
it for posterity.

Alexander Smith, *Dreamthorp*

LARGE and conspicuous, trees are a landscape's most prominent
feature and deserve to be treated with respect. The character of
an old, twisted oak or elm seldom can be duplicated within one's
lifetime. Fortunately, developers have become aware of the mone-
tary value of tree-studded lots and often will go to pains to leave
standing the more distinguished specimens.

Before planting a new tree, plan carefully. Nothing reveals an
amateur's approach like a tree planted dead center in the front
lawn. Such trees always look as though they have been planted
out of obligation. A group of three or four small trees planted off-
center or on a corner of the property can be far more effective
visually.

When planning your tree selection, consider first the function
the tree is to perform. Do you want shade, privacy, or a pleasant
accent to break the monotony of too large an expanse of lawn?
Think also of the shape and year-round appearance. You may wish
to introduce color or variety to a design that is predominantly evergreen or deciduous. And for gardeners who wish to give the required time and attention, unexcelled quality, economy, and pride
are the benefits of producing one's own fruit.

An oft-overlooked factor—perhaps because we no longer stay
in one place very long—is scale. A tree planted for quick shade
cover may rapidly become too large for its house or lot. Height and
growth rate should be fitted into your planning equation.

It's hard to keep all points in mind, and certainly trade-offs
must be made, but it is much better to be aware of what can happen than to be taken completely by surprise.

Shade and Ornamental Trees

While the distinction between a large shrub and a small tree can grow rather fine, we think of trees as plants with single trunks that attain a height of at least fifteen feet. However, even with so broad a definition, exceptions do appear. Climatic and soil factors and the gardener's preference can make a difference in the form a plant will assume. For easy reference, then, we have listed here some shrubs that are sometimes used as trees; their descriptions are given in the next chapter.

You will notice below that some trees that bear fruit suitable for either fresh-eating or preserves—e.g., loquat, common fig, red mulberry, and black walnut—are listed as shade and ornamental trees. We have placed these plants here because that is their primary function in Central Texas gardens.

Some Shade and Ornamental Varieties

Acacia. *See Huisache*

Aleppo Pine (*Pinus halepensis*). Nurseries sell quite a few of these evergreen trees, especially at Christmas time. The aleppo pine will tolerate heat and drought as well as windy, seaside conditions. It has light green needles and an open, rounded head and will grow to be from thirty to fifty feet tall after ten to fifteen years in the garden, where it serves as an ornamental. The aleppo needs iron additives to prevent chlorosis.

American Elm (*Ulmus americana*). This well-known and greatly admired American tree has a vaselike shape and graceful, upswept branches, which offer both shade and beauty. Although it may grow up to 120 feet tall, it is generally under 70 feet, and it grows at a moderate rate. It has dark green leaves three to five inches long, which turn yellow in the fall. In some areas of the country, these deciduous trees have been destroyed by a fungus known as Dutch elm disease; however, this area has to date been unaffected.

American Plane Tree. *See Sycamore*

Arizona Ash (*Fraxinus velutina*). A popular deciduous tree, this ash is slender in appearance, fast growing, and generally under its maximum height of fifty feet. It has four- to five-inch compound leaves and is a frequent choice as a shade tree.

Arizona Cypress (*Cupressus arizonica*). This native evergreen of the Southwest has scalelike foliage similar to that of the red cedar. Its silver-gray bloom makes the young tree attractive. However, when crushed, the leaves have a strong odor. In its youth, this cypress has a dense, conical crown, but it changes shape as the branches spread with age. Usually twenty to forty feet at maturity, it is rapid-growing and long-lived.

Ash. *See Arizona Ash*

Bald Cypress (*Taxodium distichum*). A regal denizen of Big Thicket and other moist environs, this deciduous conifer now is appearing at Austin shopping malls and on the city streets of Fort Worth, as landscape architects discover its adaptability to a range of conditions. Tall and conically shaped with wide, drooping branches, its pale green, feathery foliage, which turns red-orange in the fall, adds color and textural variety to any setting. It grows at a moderate rate to about 130 feet.

Blackjack Oak (*Quercus marilandica*). Often found bravely standing alone in soils too poor for other trees, this slow-growing, medium-sized oak is best identified by its wedge-shaped, leathery leaves and very rough, almost black bark. The hard, stout branches of this deciduous native form a rounded crown, giving the tree a symmetrical appearance.

Black Locust (*Robinia pseudoacacia*). Although this ornamental tree has graceful, white, fragrant flowers in late spring, its sharp thorns, its need for deep, well-drained, moist soil, and its susceptibility to locust borers make it less than satisfactory for our area. Rapidly growing to seventy-five feet, it is upright, with an open habit. Its long, feathery compound leaves are pleasing to the eye.

Black Walnut (*Juglans nigra*). This tree is more commonly found on rich bottomlands and moist, fertile hillsides than in Central or West Texas, where its relative, the **Texas Walnut** or **Little Walnut** (*J. microcarpa*) grows. The black walnut has a rounded crown, pinnately compound deciduous leaves, and sweet edible nuts. Its grows to 150 feet and is a good shade tree.

Boxelder (*Acer negundo*). The only maple with compound leaves native to Texas has become popular as a fast-growing shade tree. Deciduous and of medium height (circa forty feet), this tree is wide spreading with a curved crown. The wood of the boxelder is weak and prone to splitting. For this reason, it is not recommended.

Bradford Pear (*Pyrus calleryana* var. *Bradford*). Masses of snowy white flowers in spring and crimson leaves in fall make this deciduous, nonbearing ornamental an excellent choice. Its upward-growing branches and narrow habit are ideal for smaller areas. It will grow to its maximum height of twenty-five feet at a moderate rate.

Buckeye. *See Mexican Buckeye*

Bumelia Woollybucket (*B. lanuginosa*). The stout branches of this irregularly shaped native evergreen are covered with thick, leathery, dark green leaves with soft, woolly undersides. Drought- and insect-resistant, it is often multitrunked and, at a moderate rate of growth, will reach twenty-four feet. The black fruit, which ripens in fall, is recommended for wildlife only.

Bur Oak (*Quercus macrocarpa*). A friend at Austin's Natural Science Center gave us one of the large, distinctive acorns from which this native, deciduous shade tree gets it species name, *macrocarpa*. A high-branched tree with heavy, spreading limbs, the bur oak has a broad crown and simple alternate leaves with five to nine lobes. Growing at a medium rate to a height of up to 150 feet, the bur oak is difficult to transplant but well worth owning.

Catalpa (*C. speciosa*). Because of its enormous (six to ten inches) simple leaves and long (eight to sixteen inches) seed pods, which remain on the tree during winter, this deciduous native is easy to identify. Conspicuous clusters of white flowers with purple or yellow make it a desirable spring-blooming tree. Its height of up to fifty feet and its large features make it a suitable tree for a large yard. Susceptible to worm and insect infestations, the catalpa may require care if it is to live a long life.

Cedar. *See Deodar Cedar; Eastern Red Cedar*

Cedar Elm (*Ulmus crassifolia*). A possessor of a straight trunk and graceful branches, the region's most common elm is prized as a hearty shade provider and a handsome specimen tree. Slow-growing, the deciduous native can attain a height of ninety feet, but it

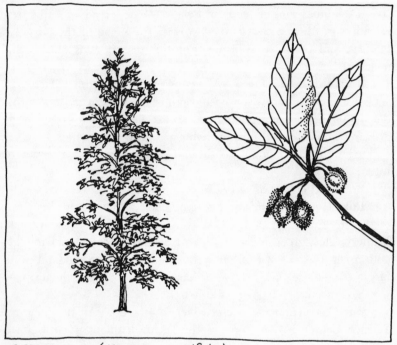

CEDAR ELM (Ulmus crassifolia)

is often much shorter in the limestone hills of Central Texas. It has small, oval leaves with serrated margins.

Chinaberry (*Melia azedarach*). Widely spreading branches and dark brown bark characterize this popular and attractive specimen. Masses of purple flowers appear in early spring, and in the fall its yellow, globular, but inedible fruit makes it very easy to identify. An Asian native with deciduous compound leaves, the chinaberry is a successful garden escape, which can be seen frequently on roadsides in urban and suburban areas. Growing at a moderate rate, it will attain a height of forty-five feet.

Chinese Arborvitae. *See shrubs, chapter 9*

Chinese Parasol Tree, also called **Varnish Tree** (*Firmiana simplex*). This is a good lawn and shade tree with large, three- to five-lobed leaves, green bark, and unusual fruit—small, pealike seeds protected by five leafy pods. This round-shaped Oriental native will grow quickly up to thirty-five feet tall. It is deciduous.

Chinese Pistachio (*Pistacia chinensis*). Its capacity to withstand both heat and drought makes this broadly spreading Chinese plant a good shade selection for our area. It is rapid growing and deciduous and has compound leaves that give fall color. It will reach up to fifty feet in height and is also used as grafting stock for the growth of pistachio nuts.

Chinese Tallow (*Sapium sebiferum*). Brilliant red color in the fall makes this medium-sized, irregularly shaped, fast-growing Oriental native a decorative addition to the home lawn. The deciduous leaves are egg shaped and have long, pointed ends. The fruit capsules contain three white seeds with vegetable tallow or wax, from which the tree gets its species name, *sebiferum*.

Common Fig (*Ficus carica*). A native of western Asia, the fig has been cultivated for its fruit here; this species, however, is grown primarily as an ornamental. It is fast-growing and may reach up to thirty feet in four years. It spreads in shrublike fashion and has deciduous leaves, which are four to eight inches long, with three to seven lobes. Varieties cultivated primarily for fruit production are listed in the fruit tree section below.

Common Hackberry (*Celtis occidentalis*). Few kind words have been spoken or written about this persistent native. Being a willing host to numerous diseases and insect pests, it rarely presents a healthy appearance. Easily identified by its warty bark, the hackberry produces a dark purple fruit relished by many bird species. The **Sugar Hackberry** (*C. laevigata*) is abundant in our region. Growing rapidly, specimens can attain a height of 120 feet. This deciduous shade tree has light green leaves and a roundish shape.

Cottonwood. *See Eastern Cottonwood*

Crabapple. *See Eley Purple Crabapple*

Crape Myrtle. *See shrubs, chapter 9*

Cypress. *See Arizona Cypress; Bald Cypress; Italian Cypress*

Deodar Cedar (*Cedrus deodara*). A dramatic example of this graceful evergreen is found in front of Littlefield House on the University of Texas campus in Austin. Originally from the Himalayas, it has a broad, conical shape, branches that droop at the tips, and blue-green, needlelike foliage, which is soft to the touch. It grows at a medium rate, and a hundred-foot specimen makes a very impressive ornamental tree.

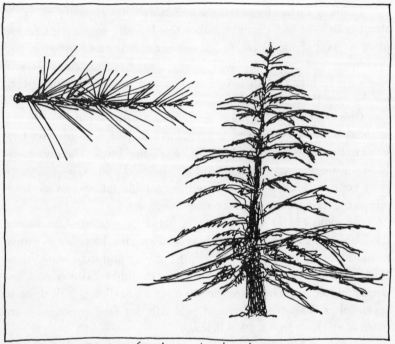

DEODAR CEDAR (Cedrus deodara)

Dogwood (*Cornus* spp.). The species (*C. florida*) so prized for its white and pink blossoms is a native of East Texas, where it is most often found in rich, moist soil under the protection of a tall pine or oak. It will survive in Central Texas if planted in rich, acid soil, kept moist, and given adequate shade. *Cornus florida* is a species that grows at a moderate rate to forty feet. Its deciduous, oval leaves are shiny on top and paler underneath. It has a spreading habit with a flat crown. The **Rough-leaf Dogwood** (*C. drummondii*) is a shrub or small tree indigenous to Central Texas. While its white flowers are comparatively inconspicuous, in late summer it produces a fruit that is relished by at least forty bird species.

Double Flowering Peach (*Prunus persica*). This is a small but striking specimen when its double flowers (white, red, or variegated) appear in spring. Its small, narrow leaves are deciduous. This fast-growing, ornamental peach tree has a broad, rounded crown.

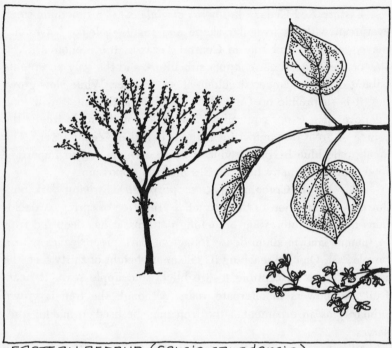

EASTERN REDBUD (Cercis canadensis)

Eastern Cottonwood (*Populus deltoides*). This large native tree likes to be near water and grows fast, but it sheds its leaves earlier than desirable. Its leaves are heart-shaped, with serrated edges, and tend to clutter lawns. Large roots that appear on top of the ground are also detracting. Despite these drawbacks, the cottonwood is attractive; it has a shimmering effect, and its leaves rustle in the breeze. Air-borne seeds of the female are regarded as a nuisance. If possible, plant male trees only.

Eastern Redbud (*Cercis canadensis*). Central Texas' favorite spring harbinger displays masses of rose-purple flowers late in winter or early in spring, before it leafs out. Broadly spreading trees with dull green, oval leaves, mature redbuds are good shade providers, although they are planted most often for their early spring blossoms. Rarely growing more than forty feet, this deciduous native is a good size for any yard and is readily available at nurseries.

Eastern Red Cedar (*Juniperus virginiana*). This medium-small evergreen with an irregular shape and small, scalelike leaves has played an important role in Central Texas as the economic main-stay of the Texas cedar-chopper subculture and the only acceptable habitat of the endangered golden-cheek warbler. While slow-growing, it is so prolific on Central Texas rangelands that it will soon take over if it is not controlled. The pollen of the male tree is the source of great discomfort for many sufferers of "cedar fever." The small, pale blue berries produced by the female are an important food source for many bird species and the oppossum.

Eley Purple Crabapple (*Malus purpurea*). Striking dark pink flowers call attention to this attractive fruit tree in spring. A decid-uous tree with interesting branching patterns, it has deep red fruit in summer and medium-dense foliage of dark green leaves with a purple cast. Quickly reaching its maximum height of thirty feet, the Eley variety is susceptible to fire blight and apple scab. It bears fruit and flowers in alternate years. Although the tree is grown primarily as an ornamental, the fruit may be used in making pre-serves.

Elm. *See American Elm; Cedar Elm; Siberian Elm*

Fig. *See Common Fig*

Fruitless Mulberry (*Morus alba*). While almost never failing to fulfill its promise as a quick shade provider, the fruitless mul-berry is not without its drawbacks. During dry spells it will shed its large, deciduous leaves as early as August. Many prefer to con-trol its rangy growth by topping the main branches during dor-mancy. This practice results in a more pleasing, bushy appearance. Left on its own, it will rapidly reach fifty feet.

Gingko, also called **Maidenhair Tree** (*G. biloba*). While this tree prefers a more temperate climate, there are specimens in our area. Another Chinese native, the deciduous gingko has been in this country since the eighteenth century. *Biloba* refers to the two-lobed leaves, which resemble those of the maidenhair fern. The pale yellow fruit is highly prized food in China and Japan; how-ever, the female fruits have an unpleasant odor. The tree is grown primarily as an ornamental in this country. Known to reach one hundred feet, it is usually under thirty feet tall. While full and round-headed in its maturity, it has a gawky yet interesting branching habit during its first twenty years.

Goldenrain Tree. *See Panicled Goldenrain Tree*

Guadalupe Palm (*Erythea edulis*). Thriving in areas with temperatures from subfreezing to desert heat, this upright fan palm from Mexico is excellent as a specimen tree or as a filler in a shrubbery design. Unlike that of many other palms, its fan-shaped foliage remains green year-round. This palm grows slowly to thirty feet.

Hackberry. *See Common Hackberry*

Honey Locust (*Gleditsia triacanthos*). Often identified by the sharp, shiny, brown thorns on the bark, this native ornamental tree grows well in a variety of climatic and soil conditions. It has a loose, open crown, with deciduous leaves, which are pinnate or featherlike and have fifteen to thirty leaflets. Varieties without thorns or seedpods are available. A moderate grower, the honey locust will reach thirty to forty feet in height.

Honey Mesquite (*Prosopis glandulosa*). The word mesquite evokes for many the image of scrubby bushes invading rangeland; while this is an accurate vision as far as it goes, the mesquite is far more versatile in its habit. A handsome accent tree with delicate, fernlike foliage, this deciduous legume contrasts well next to broad-leaf plants. Its craggy, drooping branches begin a short distance above ground, giving the mesquite a shrubby appearance. A slow grower, it will reach thirty feet.

Huisache, also called **Acacia**, **Sweet Acacia** (*A. farnesiana*). When found near the coast, the huisache is a multistemmed bush, but in Central and North Central Texas, its most common form is a single-trunk tree of up to twenty feet. Thorny branches, extremely fragrant yellow flowers, and feathery compound leaves are its outstanding features. A popular ornamental in tropical and subtropical countries, this fast-growing, deciduous native allows an economic use of every part.

Italian Cypress (*Cupressus sempervirens*). The slender evergreen of Italian Renaissance paintings is still a popular favorite in the southern part of the United States. A narrow column of a tree, its graceful and distinctive appearance makes it a desirable ornamental tree in a variety of landscapes. Its leaves are scalelike. A moderate grower, it will stand thirty to forty feet at maturity.

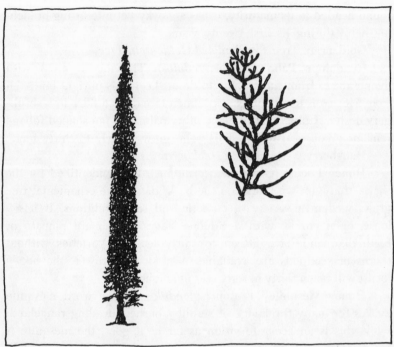

ITALIAN CYPRESS (Cupressus sempervirens)

Japanese Black Pine (*Pinus thunbergii*). This pine is an imported evergreen that has won praise for its vivid green foliage and irregular branching, which give it eye appeal and character. With the addition of soil acidifiers and iron, it does well in our area. Although the tree is slow growing, some of the older specimens are over ninety feet tall. It has medium-length needles and produces a small cone.

Jelly Palm (*Butia capitata*). This ornamental South American native is known as the jelly palm because its fruits, which appear in very abundant clusters weighing as much as seventy-five pounds, are often used for jelly. The pinnate or featherlike fronds arch dramatically and curve back toward the trunk. The evergreen *Butia* has a silvery blue cast and a short trunk, which is slow growing and will reach ten feet.

Jerusalem Thorn. *See Retama*
Ligustrum. *See shrubs, chapter 9*

LIVE OAK (Quercus virginiana)

Live Oak (*Quercus virginiana*). Perhaps no other tree better expresses the rugged beauty of its native land than this popular evergreen. The best examples have massive, low branches and dramatic, wide-spreading crowns. The live oak, which grows slowly, will eventually get up to sixty feet and is an excellent shade provider. Its small leaves make very fine mulch and additions to the compost pile. Since these are fairly expensive in nurseries, the homeowner who finds them on site should make every effort to keep and preserve them.

Loblolly Pine (*Pinus taeda*). The tall yellow pine of the famed "Lost Pines" of Bastrop County has been cultivated for lumber in the United States since 1713. The evergreen loblolly pine grows rapidly in sandy soils and has a bushy form when grown in the open. Fast-growing to 150 feet, it is good for either ornament or shade. Loblolly needles are six to nine inches long.

Locust. *See Black Locust; Honey Locust*

Lombardy Poplar (*Populus nigra* var. *italica*). A fast-growing, short-lived, deciduous tree, the poplar can be used as a screen or windbreak and may reach ninety feet. Its leaves are wedge shaped. Like the Italian cypress, it is a columnar tree, whose branches turn up and grow close to the trunk. Unfortunately, it is apt to acquire cankers as it grows, which will leave the top of the tree dead (see chapter 13).

Loquat (*Eriobotrya japonica*). Handsome and fast-growing, this broad-leaf, evergreen native of Asia produces clusters of aromatic flowers, August through November. Of medium height, it is good-looking in almost any yard. Its edible fruit makes a delicious, mild-tasting preserve. Bees attracted by the flowers may be a concern to some. The loquat's slightly triangular habit is often concealed by the variety of pruning styles to which it is subjected because of its high tolerance to heavy pruning.

Madrone. *See Texas Madrone*

Magolia. *See Southern Magnolia*

Maidenhair Tree. *See Gingko*

Maple. *See Silver Maple*

Mesquite. *See Honey Mesquite*

Mexican Buckeye (*Ungnadia speciosa*). Its persistence in limestone crevices and other difficult places make this small (to thirty feet), deciduous native with a bushy appearance a desirable specimen plant where others refuse to grow. Peachlike or redbudlike blossoms in spring are followed by a distinctive three-valved seedpod in late summer or fall. If eaten, the mildly poisonous seeds can cause stomach disturbances. The leaves of this slow-growing tree are dark green, compound, and five to twelve inches long.

Mexican Plum (*Prunus mexicana*). A small, deciduous tree, this plum is a Southwestern native and has an irregular, open crown. It has white flowers about an inch in diameter, light green, gently serrated leaves, and dark purplish red fruit, which varies in quality. Growing at a moderate rate to about twenty-five feet, it is primarily an accent tree.

Mimosa (*Albizia julibrissin*). Fernlike leaves, conspicuous masses of delicate pink flowers in May through June, and a broad, open crown are distinguishing characteristics of this popular, decid-

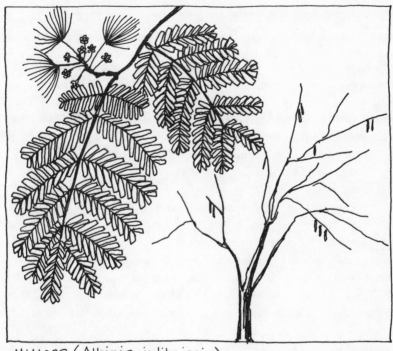

MIMOSA (Albizia julibrissin)

uous accent tree. Mimosa wilt, a fungus that causes leaves to yellow and wilt and ultimately brings about the death of the tree, can be a problem. This oriental native will rapidly achieve its maximum height of twenty feet.

Mulberry. *See Fruitless Mulberry; Red Mulberry*

Oak. *See Blackjack Oak; Bur Oak; Live Oak; Post Oak; Spanish Oak*

Olive. *See Russian Olive*

Ornamental Date Palm (*Phoenix canariensis*). Given rich, moist soil, this handsome, hardy feather palm will grow from six to twelve inches a year until it reaches about twenty feet. Its straight, erect trunk is crowned by glossy, dark green leaves, giving the neatest of evergreen palms a stately appearance.

Palm. *See Guadalupe Palm; Jelly Palm; Ornamental Date Palm; Sago Palm; Texas Palmetto; Washington Palm; Windmill Palm*

Palo Verde. *See Retama*

Panicled Goldenrain Tree (*Koelreuteria paniculata*). This is a particularly interesting tree in late summer and early fall because of its long, flowing clusters of yellow flowers, which are followed by the appearance of pinkish, bladder-shaped pods. This native of China and Japan is on the small side (under twenty feet tall) and grows fast. It is sparingly branched and deciduous and has long, compound leaves with toothed margins.

Parasol Tree. *See Chinese Parasol Tree*

Peach. *See Double Flowering Peach*

Pear. *See Bradford Pear*

Pecan (*Carya illinoinensis*). Towering and regal, our Texas state tree is valued for its dignified bearing as well as its nut production. The largest member of the hickory family, this handsome shade tree can grow to 150 feet. It is a fast-growing, deciduous tree with long (9 to 20 inches), dark, compound leaves. The fruit, which ripens in September to October, is smaller and has a harder shell than the familiar papershell commercial varieties (for nut-bearing varieties suitable for our area, see "Fruit and Nut Varieties," at the end of this section).

Persimmon. *See Texas Persimmon*

Pine. *See Aleppo Pine; Japanese Pine; Loblolly Pine; Slash Pine*

Pistachio. *See Chinese Pistachio*

Plane Tree. *See Sycamore*

Plum. *See Mexican Plum; Purple Plum*

Poplar. *See Lombardy Poplar; Silver Poplar*

Post Oak (*Quercus stellata*). Post oak is a good, hardy shade tree with stout limbs and a dense, round head. It slowly grows up to seventy-five feet tall and has deciduous, five-lobed leaves. Its acorns, which are eaten by deer and wild turkey, are set in a cup and ripen in the fall. Its rugged exterior belies an inherent fragility that prevents it from tolerating construction damage or surviving transplanting.

Purple Plum (*Prunus cerasifera*). A small ornamental, popular for its purplish foliage, this is a slow-growing tree, which, when it blooms in the spring, has delicate pink blossoms. Its large, deep purple leaves are deciduous. It has a narrow shape, with branches beginning close to the ground.

Redbud. *See Eastern Redbud*

Red Mulberry (*Morus rubra*). A small native tree (under fifty feet) with a spreading crown, it has alternate, toothed leaves, three to five inches long, which are sometimes mitten shaped or lobed. Its bark is dark gray-brown, and its sweet, edible fruit is purple or black when ripe but does not keep well. Fast-growing, it is best planted as an ornamental away from sidewalks and drives, where the falling fruit would be a nuisance.

Retama, also called **Palo Verde, Jerusalem Thorn** (*Parkinsonia aculeata*). Depending on humidity conditions, this interesting deciduous native may bloom up to five times a season, making it a good ornamental. Growing rapidly to thirty feet, the tree has delicate compound leaves that cover its widely spreading branches. When young, the tree has a green bark, which makes it easy to identify.

Russian Olive (*Elaeagnus angustifolia*). Drought- and insect-resistant, this small, deciduous tree is prized for its narrow, silvery leaves and its rapid growth. Freely spreading, it begins to branch near the ground. Growing well in all areas of Texas, it bears tan fruit in late summer and fall, which attracts many bird species.

Sago Palm (*Cycas revoluta*). Since it is slow growing, the sago palm takes fifty years to make a trunk five feet tall. Most sagos seen in landscape designs show long, dark, fernlike leaves growing from a shallow base. This makes a good accent plant for a sheltered spot.

Shumard Oak. *See Spanish Oak*

Siberian Elm (*Ulmus pumila*). Smaller than the American and cedar elms (growing to only seventy-five feet), this popular shade tree possesses virtues that include drought tolerance, rapid growth, and gracefully drooping branches. Watch for the weeping or wet joints that indicate slime flux, a bacterial disease. This condition can be corrected by installing a tap to draw off the excess fluids, which prevents the limbs from breaking. The leaves of this elm are dark green ovals, with serrated edges.

Silver Maple (*Acer saccharinum*). A water lover that grows fast and may reach a hundred feet under optimal conditions, this

maple is usually half that size in our area. This deciduous east
Texas native has five-lobed, light green leaves that are silver-white
underneath. Its wide-spreading branches provide abundant shade.
It is susceptible to insects and fungus disease and may suffer from
leaf scorch and chlorosis here. Maple fans still find much to recommend it.

Silver Poplar, also called **White Poplar** (*Populus alba*). Well-
adapted to many soils and fast-growing, this popular, deciduous
shade tree has dark green leaves with pleasantly contrasting white
undersides. The silver poplar is a tall tree, attaining a height of 100
feet.

Slash Pine (*Pinus elliottii*). Tall (up to one hundred feet),
fast-growing, inexpensive, and resistant to insect invasions, this
long-needled evergreen is a favorite with East Texas lumbermen as
well as homeowners in areas with acid soils. Regular applications
of chelated iron or iron sulphate will be necessary if chlorosis is
to be avoided in areas where soils are predominantly alkaline.

SOUTHERN MAGNOLIA (Magnolia grandiflora)

Soapberry. *See Western Soapberry*

Southern Magnolia (*M. grandiflora*). By any definition a glorious specimen tree, the southern magnolia is a large tree (up to 135 feet but normally under 50) of noble stature. It begins branching near the base of the trunk and has large, waxy evergreen leaves and extravagant blossoms. Although it naturally prefers the moist soils of east Texas, it is successfully cultivated in our area. Slow growing, it does best planted in peat. Magnolias drop their leaves at the end of their second year; this natural occurrence should not be a cause for alarm.

Spanish Oak, also called **Shumard Oak** (*Quercus shumardii*). Fall's best color comes in an attractive, deciduous native tree with symmetrical leaf design and stout, spreading branches that offer abundant shade. A medium to large tree depending on the area, it is a beauty, and, additionally, it is fairly free from insects and diseases. Although slow compared with Chinese tallow or Arizona ash, it is one of the faster-growing oaks.

Sycamore, also called **American Plane Tree** (*Platanus occidentalis*). Tall, conical, and rapid-growing, this deciduous native is one of the most popular shade trees. It has broadly lobed, simple leaves, four to twelve inches across. The sycamore's size can be overpowering for small yards, and in alkaline soils iron chlorosis is a treatable but common problem.

Tallow. *See Chinese Tallow*

Texas Madrone (*Arbutus texana*). A beautiful, small native found on the Edwards Plateau and westward but now on the verge of extinction, the madrone is sometimes known as the **Naked Indian** for its smooth, pink bark. Dark green leaves provide a striking background for the bright red berries that appear on this evergreen in the fall and winter. Its widely branching trunk and crooked limbs give it a shrublike appearance. Although difficult to transplant, it can be started from seed collected in November and December. It grows very slowly.

Texas Mountain Laurel. *See shrubs, chapter 9*

Texas Palmetto (*Sabal texana*). At home along the Rio Grande River, this tropical-appearing evergreen may reach 20 to 40 feet in height with a trunk 1½ to 3 feet in diameter. Its fan-shaped leaves are 3 to 5 feet wide and are long. Like other sabals, the ornamental *texana* has a distinctive leaf, which is split down the middle, supposedly to make it wind resistant. The dead fronds on this and other palms should be removed for a neat appearance. While easy to propagate from seed, it is difficult to transplant.

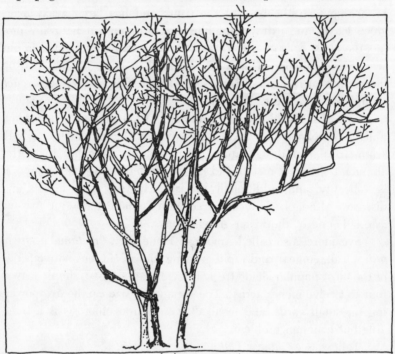

TEXAS PERSIMMON (Diospyros texana)

Texas Persimmon (*Diospyros texana*). Slight and delicate with smooth, gray bark and intricate branching patterns, the deciduous native persimmon has small, leathery leaves and is a desirable accent tree. Its black fruit is appreciated by a variety of birds and mammals. A slow grower, this small tree looks best when not overshadowed by larger shade trees.

Tree-of-Heaven (*Ailanthus altissima*). A rapid-growing, hardy specimen, this tree has gained popularity in urban areas due to its ability to thrive in spite of dust, smoke, and poor soil. It reaches sixty feet in height. A native of China, it has deciduous compound leaves with eleven to forty-one leaflets, which give it a tropical appearance. Bruised leaves and male flowers have an unpleasant odor.

Vitex. *See shrubs, chapter 9*

Walnut. *See Black Walnut*

Washington Palm (*Washingtonia filifera* and *Washingtonia robusta*). Dedicated to President George Washington, the W. *filifera* is a native of the Southwest, while the W. *robusta* is the Mexican

WEEPING WILLOW (Salix babylonica)

species. They are similar, although, according to one local palm expert we know, the *filifera* is hardier and less likely to freeze. This striking ornamental evergreen grows at a moderate rate into a tall tree (forty feet or more), with a cylindrical trunk up to three feet wide, which is often covered with dead pendant leaves that form a large skirt. The fan-shaped leaves are up to six feet long and five feet across. This palm has small, black, berrylike fruit. There are many fine specimens at the Alamo.

Weeping Willow (*Salix babylonica*). A romantic-looking import from China, this willow is characterized by drooping branches. This fast-growing deciduous tree may reach fifty feet in height. It does best when there is water nearby. It is subject to insect borers. A curly-leaf variety (**corkscrew willow**) that is very attractive is sometimes available.

Western Soapberry (*Sapindus drummodii*). This deciduous native, growing to fifty feet, is frequently confused with the chinaberry. A good shade tee, it is slender, with a rounded head. It has long, yellowish green, compound leaves and produces an abundance of white flowers in early spring. The fruit has been used to make soap in Mexico.

White Poplar. *See Silver Poplar*
Willow. *See Weeping Willow*

WINDMILL PALM (Trachycarpus fortunei)

Windmill Palm (*Trachycarpus fortunei*). This deciduous native of China owes its common name to windmill-like, fan-shaped leaves, about three feet in diameter, with stiff, dark green leaflets. One of the hardiest of all palms, it appears to prefer the cooler climates, although it can be grown in our area. Under good conditions, it will grow six inches or more a year, reaching a height of fifteen to thirty-five feet. The hairy appearance of the trunk comes from a thick mass of long, dark fibers growing from the leaf base. This is the only palm recommended for the Dallas–Fort Worth area.

Woollybucket. *See Bumelia Woollybucket*
Yaupon. *See shrubs, chapter 9*

Fruit and Nut Trees

Full sun, good drainage, and soil high in humus all are crucial to good fruit production, but the single most important condition is the "chilling factor," or the number of hours below forty-five degrees Fahrenheit needed to set fruit. Because most fruit trees require 700 hours, a number most of Central Texas cannot count on achieving, selection of varieties proven to produce in our climate is essential. Always buy your trees locally; never purchase from the tempting, glossy Sunday newspaper supplements. The difference of 100 hours in the chilling factor between Central and North Central Texas means that growing apples and cherries is possible in the Dallas–Fort Worth area and its surrounding counties. While there are those who will argue that it is possible to grow apples in Central Texas (650 hours average chilling factor in Travis County), reliable and consistent crops are doubtful and the quality of fruit poor.

Instructions for pruning, fertilizing, and spraying are specific for a given fruit and area. The county extension agents are the best sources for continuously updated material.

Following is a list of fruit trees well adapted to the climate of Central Texas.

Some Fruit and Nut Varieties

Apples

Generally apples need more cold weather than we can provide. However, there are several varieties that grow here, especially in the slightly cooler northern part of our region. You will need two varieties of apples for good pollination. Here are several suggestions:

Holland. Discovered in the 1920's at Weatherford, Texas, this is a standard commercial variety, which has a relatively low chilling requirement. The fruit matures in early August, is large, has a fair red color, and bruises easily.

Molly's Delicious. Rated fair to good in fruit quality, it is a low-chilling early variety and is light red.

Starbrimson Delicious. This is a late-season apple with good red color and typical red delicious shape. Its quality is rated adequate, and it has proven popular in the Dallas–Fort Worth area.

Waynespur Delicious. A relatively new, red, late-season variety, this has gotten good reports from the Texas Agricultural Experiment Station in Montague.

Cherries, Sour

Montmorency. This is a tart sour cherry, which adapts to North Central Texas, even though it has a high chilling requirement. It is a self-pollinator whose fruits require cooking.

Figs

Celeste. Thriving in all areas of Texas, the Celeste fig is a high-quality fruit for fresh eating or preserving. It ripens in late June.

Texas Everbearing. A vigorous grower, this medium-large fig of good quality ripens in late June.

Alma. Developed by the Texas Agricultural Experiment Station, the alma is productive and yields a high-quality fruit in late June.

Peaches

Springold. A good early variety, the springold produces a small clingstone with yellow flesh. It ripens the end of May.

Sam Houston. This large freestone is a popular garden variety but is not used commercially because of its susceptibility to bacterial spot. A low-chilling variety, it ripens in mid-June.

Sentinel. An extremely productive tree, the Sentinel yields a good quality semi-freestone in mid-June.

Keystone. This is a popular Hill Country commercial variety. Its fruit, large and sweet, ripens in June.

Loring. Resistant to bacterial spot, the Loring is a popular commercial variety. Its fruit is large and of good quality.

Dixieland. A large freestone of excellent quality, this moderately bacterial spot–resistant variety ripens in mid-July.

Frank. Excellent for canning and freezing, the Frank has been producing consistent crops in Texas since the turn of the century. The fruit, a good-textured clingstone, ripens in August.

Hale Haven. This is a good producer of excellent eating fruit for the area north of Waco. It ripens in early June.

Ranger. A dependable commercial producer in north and west Texas, Ranger gives high yields of large-sized fruit in late June.

Redglobe. Another variety best suited to the northern areas of our region, this attractive tree produces good-quality fruit in early June.

Pears

Orient. This is the most fire blight–resistant of the pears suitable for the Central Texas area. The fruit is better for canning than as a fresh fruit. It requires a pollinator.

Moonglow. Producing a mild-flavored fruit at an early age, it is less gritty than many of the other varieties and is considered good as a table fruit as well as for processing. It is also a good pollinator for other varieties.

Keiffer. A popular home-yard pear, it boasts high resistance to fire blight. It requires a pollinator. The fruit is used mostly for preserves, as it is quite gritty.

Maxine. It produces a good fresh-fruit pear and does well in Central Texas conditions. It requires a pollinator.

Pecans

Desirable. A leading commercial (improved papershell) producer, Desirable yields a quality nut and is relatively disease-resistant. The tree will bear in eight years.

Choctaw. It produces a large, good-quality papershell nut after eight years and is relatively disease-resistant.

Cheyenne. With a medium-sized papershell nut, it is a highly productive tree after eight years.

Mohawk. This comes into production at six years and produces a large papershell nut whose quality is fair to good.

Caddo. Caddo produces a small, good-quality papershell nut at six years. It is a strong tree, which is disease-resistant.

Shawnee. It produces a good-quality, medium-sized papershell nut at eight years.

Sioux. This yields a small papershell nut of excellent quality.

Persimmons, Japanese

Eureka. This variety consistently produces a heavy fruit of good quality.

Hachiya. Large, seedless, cone-shaped fruit are produced by this variety.

Tamopan. A moderate producer, the Tamopan bears fruit with a distinctive constrictive ring about the middle.

Plums

Methley. Self-pollinating and a moderately vigorous grower, the Methley is a good garden variety. Ripening in early June, it produces a medium-sized fruit.

Bruce. This common commercial variety produces a large, juicy plum excellent for preserves. A pollinator is necessary for crop production.

Santa Rosa. While producing excellent-quality fruit, this short-lived self-pollinator is highly susceptible to bacterial spot and stem canker.

Ozark Premier. A high chilling requirement makes this variety suitable for only the northern area of Central Texas. The tree is strong and self-pollinating, and it produces an exceptional fruit in late June.

Shrubs: A Checklist

Everything that grows
Holds in perfection but a little moment.
Shakespeare, "Sonnet 15"

THERE are shrubs for every garden, and the real problem for the homeowner may turn out to be too many choices. Some shrubs are evergreen, giving year-round color; some are deciduous, shedding their foliage in winter. Some are chosen for their appealing blossoms or their attractive foliage. Shrubs may be used as a hedge to mark off an area, to provide a windbreak, or to offer privacy, or, more often, they may serve as the main decorative element in the garden.

Usually we think of a shrub as a woody plant that is not too tall and has many stems, while a tree has one trunk and grows to a larger size. Yet nature doesn't draw definitive lines, and there are a number of plants (such as crape myrtle and mountain laurel) that are often listed under the heading of "shrubs or small trees." The pruning shears determine which form such plants will take in the garden.

Before selecting your shrubs, you might read through the list that follows and note the main features of different bushes. Then consider the main functions of the plants to be used in a certain spot in your garden. If, for example, you are planning a shrub border, you might begin from the back and select the tallest-growing shrubs first. Be certain the ones chosen will eventually be tall enough to give the privacy you want but not so tall they will eliminate sunlight and breezes or dwarf your house or yard. Size at maturity should be one of your most important considerations. Most of the time six- to eight-feet shrubs will do the best job.

With the tallest shrubs selected, you can fill in with smaller shrubs in front. As mentioned in chapter 4, it is generally preferable to use clusters rather than single plants in a row. If you use flowering shrubs (and we hope you will consider that), be sure to take into account blooming times and the amount of sun or shade in the planting location. If a plant requires sun, it won't blossom properly in shade, and a shade lover may be sunburned or turn brown in a site with full sun.

The decided preference for evergreen shrubs in our climate is perfectly understandable. We have a very wide selection of evergreens and semi-evergreens (plants that generally lose about half their leaves in winter) in Central Texas. Many of them are attractive and easily maintained. In addition, they offer another, more indirect benefit: on the most gloomy winter day there is some psychological reassurance in seeing a lush, green plant, oblivious to nature's extremes, thriving in the garden. Having said this, we are quick to point out that special features of some deciduous shrubs make them also very desirable. For instance, the shape and the flowers of the crape myrtle are worth a little winter barrenness.

The following list of shrubs, we hope, will prepare you to make your decisions. For other suggestions regarding shopping and selecting plants, see chapter 4.

A Checklist of Common Shrubs

Abelia (*A. grandiflora*). Preferring full sun but tolerating partial shade, this medium-sized evergreen with graceful, arching branches produces white-pink flowers from early summer to fall. Enduring a wide range of conditions, the abelia is also versatile in function, serving equally well as a hedge or a specimen shrub. In fall its simple, opposite leaves take on a bronze cast. Dwarf varieties are available.

Agarita, also called **Laredo Mahonia** (*Berberis trifoliolata*). An interesting evergreen native with stiff, slightly variegated, holly-shaped leaves, the agarita is a medium-sized shrub that thrives in Hill Country soils, in sun or shade. It does equally well as a specimen or a hedge. The bright red berries that appear in spring are excellent for preserves or for attracting birds. Because its leaves are sharp and thorny, it should be planted where it can do no harm to the passerby.

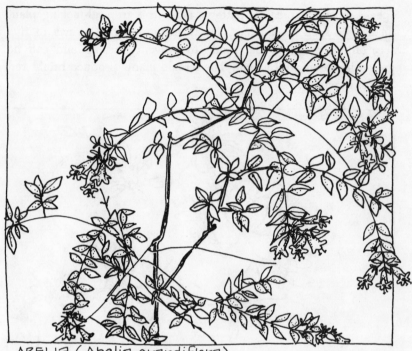

ABELIa (Abelia grandiflora)

Althea. *See Shrub Althea*

American Beautyberry, also called **French Mulberry** (*Calli-carpa americana*). This deciduous North American native owes its popularity to the extravagant profusion of purple berries growing in the leaf axils from August through November. Birds and mammals are known to appreciate their taste as much as we do their beauty. Its leaves are four to six inches long, and it can grow from three to six feet tall. It is an easy plant to establish from seed or cuttings. Best as a specimen, it likes some sun.

Aralia (*A. sieboldii*). The tropical look of its large, maple-shaped leaves makes the evergreen aralia a good choice for ornamental purposes. It prefers partial or full shade, will grow to between three and six feet, and can be planted singly or in a group.

Arborvitae. *See Chinese Arborvitae*

Aucuba, also called **Gold Dust** (*Aucuba japonica*). Gold specks or variegated leaf patterns make this tropical-looking plant an easy-to-spot specimen. A hardy evergreen that grows to five feet tall, it needs partial shade to prevent burning and can be grown inside as well as out. The female plants produce bright red berries in winter.

AZaLEa (Rhododendron spp.)

Azalea (*Rhododendron* spp.). Despite its inappropriateness for our predominantly alkaline soil, there are legions who are willing to go to great lengths to enjoy the spectacular beauty of this *Rhododendron* genus of the heath family. And understandably so, for it is a flowering shrub of outstanding beauty. Masses of azaleas flourish under the live oaks at the Austin campus of the University of Texas, but not without effort, says the U.T. horticulturist we talked to. Cool, moist, acid soil is the azalea's primary demand. This means removing all soil from the hole in which the shrub is to be planted, adding peat, and then backfilling with peat only.

Moisture can be kept in, and the temperature kept down with two to three inches of mulch, preferably, a medium or fine pine mulch or oak leaves. In our severe climate, the azalea should be planted in partial shade. A balanced shrub fertilizer should be applied after the blossoms have fallen and then every six weeks until September. During very hot and dry periods, the azalea may need to be watered several times a week since the feeding roots are close to the surface.

Two evergreen species recommended for our area are the **Indica Azalea** (*R. indicum*) and the **Kurume Azalea** (*R. obtusum*). Both are available in a wide color range with single or double blossoms. The indica is a larger plant—both its leaves and its blossoms are larger. Indicas grow to 6 feet tall; their flowers are 2–3 inches across and the leaves are 1½ inches long. The kurume is hardier and has a more compact growth habit, reaching about 3–4 feet in height with flowers that are ¾–1½ inches wide.

Bamboo (*Bambusa* spp.). For a super-quick hedge that's usually evergreen or for a screening device or for places where nothing else will grow, some people choose bamboo plants. However, beware; some varieties of bamboo will take over the property if you don't chop through the rhizomes periodically. Not only will it spread but it will grow quite tall. *Bambusa multiplex*, for example, will grow to heights of twelve to fifteen feet in sun or filtered light. It often forms a compact, graceful clump; the shoots are almost two inches at the base, and the leaves are silver underneath.

Banana (*Musa paradisiaca* var. *spaientum*). Cold-hardy varieties of this South American giant will survive temperatures down to twenty-five degrees Fahrenheit but will not withstand prolonged periods of subfreezing weather. Evergreen in its native environment, it may freeze back in harsh winters. It should be planted only in the southern part of Central Texas. There it should be planted in a sheltered spot, protected from wind, which can shred its leaves. Not only are the tattered leaves unsightly, but they are less productive in manufacturing food to maintain growth. A heavy nitrogen user, the banana prefers deep soil, rich in humus. Banana trees planted along San Antonio's famed River Walk produce bountiful clusters of fruit.

Barbados Cherry (*Malpighia glabra*). This shrub from the West Indies is not as popular as many others in our area, according to nurseries. It has pink- to rose-colored flowers that bloom throughout the summer and produce bright red, three-lobed, cherrylike fruit that has a high vitamin content and makes good jelly.

Barberry. *See Crimson Pigmy Barberry*

Bluebeard, also called **Blue Spirea** (*Caryopteris incana*). A deciduous woody shrub from the Orient, this plant offers as its primary feature small, summer-blooming, violet-blue flowers, produced in "spires" from which it gets one of its names. It has opposite, toothed leaves and will reach a height of five feet. It should be grown in a flower bed or shrubbery border with lots of sun.

Blue Spirea. *See Bluebeard*

Bottlebrush. *See Lemon Bottlebrush*

Boxwood. *See Japanese Littleleaf Box*

CAMELLIA (Camellia japonica)

Camellia (*C.* spp.). For the past 150 years, these beautiful specimen plants have been inspiring flower lovers and homeowners in America. They can be large shrubs or small trees, and there are several hundred varieties. The soil for camellias should be well drained and rich in humus and acid. These plants are renowned not only for their flowers but also for their dark, leathery, evergreen leaves. The **Common Camellia** (*C. japonica*) has large flowers up to five inches wide, single or double, and blooms from October to April. The **Sasanqua Camellia** (*C. sasanqua*) blooms earlier, from September to December, and features smaller, less showy flowers. If you plant both species, you get a long blooming season. Although camellias like sun, a little shade in our hot climate will help prevent leaf burn. We will list only a few of the varieties available.

C. japonica:

Red—Adolph Audusson, semidouble; Aunt Jetty, double; C. M. Hovey, double (very good); Professor C. S. Sargent, double (especially hardy)

Pink—Debutante, double (good corsage); Frau Minna Seidel, double (very popular); Sweeti Vera, double (petals have red line and dots)

White—Alba Plena, double (an old variety); Amabilis, single; Purity, double (excellent corsages)

Variegated—Daikagura, double; Donckelari, semidouble (very hardy); Kermes, double (some fragrance); SaraSa, semidouble (especially popular)

C. sasanqua:

Pink—Briar Rose, single

White—Blanchette, single (pink tint on petal edges); Mino-no-yuki, double (faint scent)

Rose-colored—Hugh Evans, single; Tanya, single

Cape Plumbago (*P. capensis*). Small, pale blue flowers that bloom throughout the summer and a liking for hot, dry climates account for the popularity of this deciduous shrub. This specimen plant has lance-shaped leaves. A South African native, it is a climbing shrub, which needs full sun but requires little water.

Cenizo. *See Senisa*

Century Plant (*Agave americana*). Flowering but once after twenty years of growth, the dramatic succulent then dies. The agave, with its barbed, fleshy leaves, is a large evergreen plant at

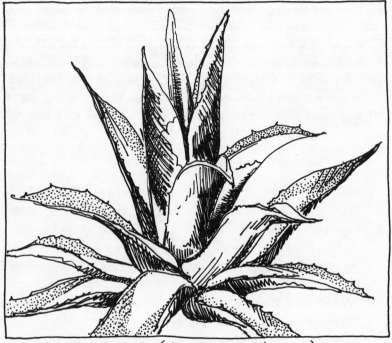

CENTURY PLANT (Agave americana)

maturity and should be given ample space and full sun when planted. The stalk, ascending to a height of twenty feet or more, resembles a giant asparagus, which then bursts open, exposing its yellow blossoms.

Cherry Laurel (*Prunus caroliniana*). A handsome, fast-growing (up to thirty feet) evergreen, native to the southeastern United States, this shrub has a rich foliage with two- to four-inch green leaves, inconspicuous white flowers, and shiny black fruit. Use it as a specimen or a hedge that will require some maintenance. Plant it in full or partial sun and shape it as you prefer.

Chinese Arborvitae (*Thuja orientalis*). Bright green, dense foliage and a formal appearance make this ten- to twenty-foot evergreen a popular landscape specimen or windscreen for stately homes. It requires plenty of sun. Spider mites and bagworms are frequent invaders.

Chinese Photinia (*P. serrulata*). This is a very popular evergreen ornamental in our area, primarily because of its long, reddish bronze leaves. It also has small, white flowers in spring and red berries in fall and winter. Another variety (*P. fraseri*) is often seen in the nurseries. Both are capable of reaching to twenty feet and will grow in sun or partial shade.

Cleyera. *See Japanese Cleyera*

Cotoneaster (*C.* spp.). The rugged appearance and high tolerance of heat and sun of these semi-evergreen shrubs give them an appropriate look in Central Texas. The **Rock Cotoneaster** (*C. horizontalis*) produces small pink flowers in spring, which are followed by red berries in fall, making this a colorful plant in most seasons. Its low, flat growth habit makes it a suitable rock garden specimen in sunny locations. The **Silverleaf Cotoneaster** (*C. pannosa*) is a vigorous grower with white flowers in spring and dull red berries in fall. Its gray-green leaves have woolly white undersides.

Crape Myrtle (*Lagerstroemia indica*). Originally from India, this commonly cultivated small tree or shrub owes much of its popularity to the many showy flowers in pink, red, purple, or white that appear in summer. Its deciduous leaves are small and shaped like inverted eggs. Crape myrtle is an attractive specimen plant, which blooms best in full sun and will grow up to twenty feet tall. We have seen it used effectively as a hedge on larger lots. Watch for powdery mildew on this plant. An old variety of crape myrtle, called **Dallas Red,** and several new varieties as well are fairly resistant to powdery mildew.

Crimson Pigmy Barberry (*Berberis thunbergii* var. *atropurpurea nana*). With thorny stems and red-purple foliage, this good-looking, compact (one to two feet tall) deciduous plant is valued for the color it adds to the landscape scheme. It is partial to sun and is especially attractive in rock gardens.

Cypress Lavendercotton. *See Santolina*

Deutzia. *See Slender Deutzia*

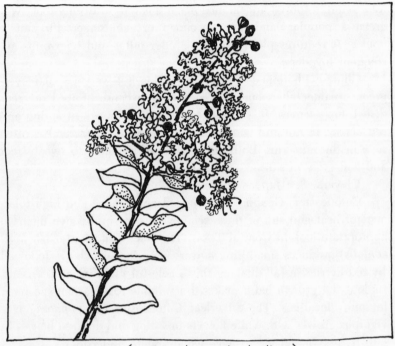

CRAPE MYRTLE (Lagerstroemia indica)

Elaeagnus. *See Thorny Elaeagnus*

Euonymus (*E.* spp.). Its susceptibility to scale and powdery mildew detracts somewhat from the many attributes of this Japenese import. It has lustrous evergreen leaves, compact growth, and a liking for either sun or shade. The **Dwarf Boxleaf** species (*E. pulchella*) makes a fine, low hedge, while the **Evergreen Euonymus** (*E. japonicus*) is often used as a specimen. Variegated varieties are available; color ranges from lustrous dark green to green rimmed with white or yellow.

Fatshedera (*F. lizei*). A curious hybrid of fatsia and English ivy, fatshedera has oversized palmately lobed leaves (seven to eleven inches across) that give it a tropical appearance. Its high tolerance for shade makes it a valuable plant for dark courtyards, areas between buildings, and other deeply shaded nooks. Fatshedera is an evergreen that grows up to seven feet and makes an interesting specimen in the garden. It roots easily from softwood cuttings.

Feijoa. *See Pineapple Guava*

Ferns. With a few exceptions, most prominently the native maidenhair, which thrives on seeping limestone outcroppings, the arid areas of Texas are not a hospitable climate for fern plants. However, if you provide moist soil high in humus content and at least partial shade, the following cultivated varieties will do quite well as specimens eighteen to thirty-six inches tall. All are evergreen here except chain fern. Once established, ferns prefer to be left undisturbed and do not require fertilizer. One caution: do not permit them to dry out.

Autumn Fern (*Dryopteris erythrosorsa*). Claret-red when very young, this Oriental native will change to bronze and eventually to a brilliant green when fully mature. Its 1- to 1½-foot fronds turn cocoa-violet in summer and fall.

Chain Fern (*Woodwardia virginica*). Attaining a height of three to four feet, the chain fern is the tallest of the recommended ferns. If you cannot provide plenty of moisture and acid soil, don't try this one. Freezing back in winter, the plant will put on new growth in spring.

Christmas Fern (*Polystichum acrostichoides*). A native of eastern Texas, the Christmas fern will tolerate more sunlight than most ferns. The dark, evergreen foliage grows from one to two feet.

Holly Fern (*Cyrtomium falcatum*). Handsome and evergreen, this fern has leathery, holly-shaped leaves and a tolerance for partial sun that make it one of our most popular ferns.

Leatherwood Fern (*Dryopteris marginalis*). Answering to a number of common names, the leatherwood demands deep soil and constant moisture. Its twenty-inch fronds are evergreen and leathery in texture.

Maidenhair Fern (*Adiantum pedatum*). Commonly seen growing on the limestone outcroppings of the Edwards Plateau, the maidenhair is one of the few ferns that prefer alkaline soil. This native, whose delicately rounded leaves are emphasized by jet black stems, requires shade and a constantly moist location.

Firethorn. *See Pyracantha*

Flowering Quince. *See Japanese Flowering Quince*

Forsythia (*F.* spp.). Heralding spring with its abundant and brilliantly yellow blossoms, the forsythia is an excellent complement to the redbud tree. While forsythia is fairly well adapted to most of Central Texas, profuse blossoms of this deciduous native of Asia are most consistent in North Central Texas. Free of most diseases and insects, the fast-growing shrub demands little care other than pruning. The natural arch of the branches should be preserved by thinning out right after the blooming period crowded branches and suckers at the base of the plant. Lynwood Gold is an excellent variety for Central Texas.

Gardenia (*G. jasminoides*). Best known for that heady, romantic fragrance that has filled so many school gymnasiums on prom

GARDENIA (Gardenia jasminoides)

night, this handsome evergreen has dark green, waxy leaves. Depending on the variety, gardenias are from three to ten feet tall. They suffer from chlorosis in this area, a problem that is compounded when they are planted along the foundation line or other masonry. To correct this condition, the plants should be given regular applications of copperas or other form of iron and acidifier. We have found that dwarf varieties require less care and are generally hardier. Gardenias will do best in sun to partial shade. In Texas, two popular varieties are the August Beauty and Mystery, both varieties of *G. jasminoides.* The August Beauty produces more abundant but smaller blossoms. Both the foliage and flowers of the Mystery are larger than those of the August Beauty. *Gardenia radicans* is an excellent dwarf variety.

Gold Dust. *See Aucuba*

Gold Flower, also called **St. John's Wort** (*Hypericum moserianum*). Blooming in partial shade, this hardy semi-evergreen is a good color candidate for those difficult places. Its masses of yellow flowers bloom steadily from summer to fall. A medium-sized shrub with stalkless leaves, it can withstand heavy pruning.

Guava. *See Pineapple Guava*

Hawthorne. *See Indian Hawthorne*

Hesperaloe. *See Red Hesperaloe*

Holly (*Ilex* spp.). Hollies are an enormously popular family due to their glossy, rectangular-shaped evergreen foliage, shade tolerance, and sturdy growth habits. Of the numerous varieties, the **Burford Holly** (*I. cornuta burfordii*) is slow-growing, and has been known to reach a height of twenty-five feet. It is heavily fruited and is also available in a dwarf variety. **Chinese** or **Horned Holly** (*I. cornuta*) is known for its large, bright red berries, which can be produced without pollen from a male plant. Three of its five spines are arranged at the apex in a hornlike manner, which accounts for one of its names. **Carissa Holly** (*I. cornuta* var. *carissa*) is a fairly recent addition to the family in dwarf size and has a most attractive dense, spreading foliage, although it does not produce berries. Hollies make fine hedge or specimen plants.

Hydrangea (*H. macrophylla*). Although it does better in richer soil, the hydrangea can be grown in our area. A deciduous plant

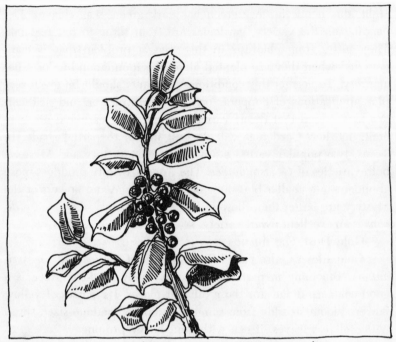

BURFORD HOLLY (Ilex cornuta burfordii)

that will reach six feet and over, it has small flowers that grow in large ten- to twelve-inch clusters and blossom in summer. Its flowers are white, pink, and blue; to produce blue blooms, add aluminum sulphate to the soil before the buds appear. Often called bigleaf hydrangea because of its four- to eight-inch leaves, it prefers partial shade and can be used as a houseplant. Prune and propagate from cuttings in the fall.

Indian Hawthorne (*Raphiolepis indica*). Dark, evergreen, leathery leaves and charming pink-white flowers in early spring define this sun-loving native of China. It will reach six feet in height and is often used as a border in spite of its irregular growth habit. Despite the plant's susceptibility to fire blight and scale, the popularity of the hawthorne is growing. To maintain a compact shape, prune after blossoms have faded. Dwarf varieties are available.

Japanese Cleyera (*C. japonica*). As one of the few shrubs that does best in shade, this medium-sized evergreen with simple, glossy leaves and small, white flowers in spring has a special value. Variegated forms with attractive white leaf margins are also available. Cleyera is a specimen plant that can be easily shaped and pruned.

Japanese Flowering Quince (*Chaenomeles japonica*). This deciduous plant belongs to a popular group of Asiatic shrubs grown mostly as specimens. *C. japonica,* which is low-growing (three feet), has bright red flowers. Its relative, *C. alpina,* has orange ones, which bloom very early, before their leaves appear. Quince needs full sun and is subject to scale; its one- to three-inch oval leaves have saw-toothed edges.

Japanese Littleleaf Box (*Buxus microphylla* var. *japonica*). A three- to six-foot shrub introduced into America from Japan in 1860, it is widely planted in the southern United States, where it seems to thrive. Its evergreen leaves are about an inch long. Its dense, compact growth, which does best in full or partial sun, and its low maintenance make it useful as a hedge.

Japanese Yew (*Podocarpus macrophyllus*). Tall, narrow, with long, needlelike leaves, this bright evergreen adds variety of texture, color, and form to many landscape plans. It commonly is used to soften the corners of buildings. It will grow in full sun to partial shade.

Jasmines. *See vines, chapter 10*

Juniper (*Juniperus* spp.). New varieties ranging greatly in color, size, and growth habit are introduced continuously by nurserymen. The juniper's popularity in our area is well deserved. It grows well in alkaline soils, tolerates intense sun, and is drought resistent. Responding well to trimming, it makes a good specimen plant in a rock garden. Left alone to follow its natural growing pattern, it is equally successful as a windscreen. With needlelike leaves, which vary from a blue-gray to a dark green, this versatile evergreen will not tolerate shade well. Two of the more popular varieties are pfitzer juniper and creeping juniper.

Kashgar Tamarisk, also called **Salt Cedar** (*Tamarix hispida*). Although the Caspian Sea region is the home of this hardy evergreen shrub, it grows well in dry soil, is medium-sized, and displays bright, pink, fluffy flowers in summer. Soft, delicate foliage gives

JAPANESE YEW (Podocarpus macrophyllus)

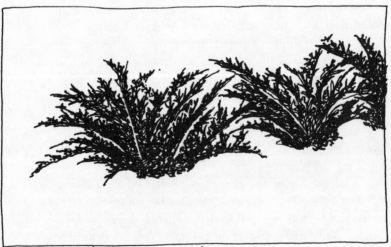

JUNIPER (Juniperus spp.)

the plant an ethereal look. Use as a specimen, and plant in sun or partial shade.

Lantana (*L. camara*). Irregularly shaped with a spreading growth habit, this cultivated close relative of the **Texas Lantana** (*L. horrida*) is a popular deciduous landscape plant throughout the South. It blooms profusely and in multicolored blossoms ranging from yellow-orange to pink-yellow to white-lilac. Its leaves are dark green and rough textured. Thriving in full sun, it is easy to grow from seed or cuttings and will get to be about four feet tall.

Laredo Mahonia. *See Agarita*

Laurel. *See Cherry Laurel; Texas Mountain Laurel*

Lavendar. *See True Lavender*

Lavender Cotton. *See Santolina*

Lemon Bottlebrush (*Callistemon lanceolatus*). Bristly spikes of crimson blossoms account for the name of this tall, evergreen Australian native. Because its lanceolate foliage is sparse, it looks best when planted in a companion setting with more dense shrubs. Thriving in dry, hot conditions, it blooms well only in full sun. Since it is semihardy, we recommend it for the southern parts of the region.

Ligustrum (*L.* spp.). **Japanese Privets** also called **Waxleaf Ligustrum** (*L. japonicum*) are popular, utilitarian evergreens with shiny, elliptical leaves. These shade-tolerant shrubs are commonly used as hedges, border plants, or specimens and grow from six to fifteen feet tall. Clusters of small, white flowers fill the air with a heady fragrance in spring. A topiary form known as **Poodle Ligustrum** (spheres of foliage separated by segments of exposed trunk, suggesting the elaborate hair clip of the French poodle) is popular with more formal architectural styles. **Glossy Privet** (*L. lucidum*) attains a height of fifteen feet. This slender and frequently multitrunked, treelike shrub is serviceable as a windbreak or screen. In May and June tiny blossoms fill the air with a heady fragrance. The bark is light gray to tan, and the semi-evergreen leaves have a pale undersurface. Well-suited to our soils and climate, it is a favorite at nurseries.

Lilac (*Syringa vulgaris*). Brought to us by the earliest American settlers, this nostalgic, gently scented deciduous plant flourishes

WaXLeaF LiGuSTRuM (Ligustrum japonicum)

(six to eight feet high) in the Dallas–Ft. Worth area. It needs good exposure to sun. Its heart-shaped leaves and lilac flowers, which bloom in spring, are widely admired. Feed it in spring and fall, cut off suckers, and watch for scale and powdery mildew.

Mahonia. *See Agarita*

Mescal Bean. *See Texas Mountain Laurel*

Mountain Laurel. *See Texas Mountain Laurel*

Mulberry. *See American Beautyberry*

Myrtle. *See True Myrtle*

Nandina (*N. domestica*). One of the more popular oriental imports, this medium-sized (three to six feet) evergreen displays large clusters of bright red fruits in the fall and winter. It has white, conspicuous flowers in the summer, and its compound, oval leaves turn red to scarlet in the fall. Nandina thrives in sun or shade and makes a fine border. It is also available in a dwarf variety (*N. d.* var. *nana purpurea*).

Oleander (*Nerium oleander*). Thriving with little attention in hot, dry situations, the oleander boasts flowers of pink, red, white,

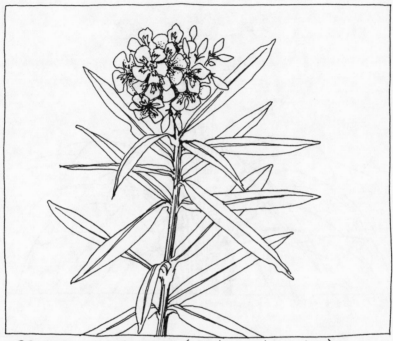

COMMON OLEANDER (Nerium oleander)

or yellow, which bloom throughout the summer. Its evergreen foliage is similar to that of the bamboo plant. It grows up to twenty feet and needs occasional root pruning. This plant is poisonous, and contact with leaves can produce dermatitis. Oleander likes a lot of sun. Semihardy, it will die back in severe cold; new growth will appear in spring.

Pampas Grass (*Cortaderia selloana*). Growing in large clumps, this tall, evergreen, grasslike shrub sends up long, showy, silver-beige plumes in fall. Its distinctive foliage and dense growth habit make it an excellent specimen plant or screen. Pampas grass likes sunshine but will tolerate some shade.

Photinia. *See Chinese Photinia*

PAMPAS GRASS (Cortaderia selloana)

Pineapple Guava, also called **Feijoa** (*Feijoa sellowiana*). This South American evergreen with oval, gray-green leaves bears exotic red and white blossoms in spring if it receives full sun. The pineapple guava makes an interesting specimen, which may grow to fifteen to twenty feet tall. An edible fruit may be produced if several bushes are planted close to one another.

Pittosporum (*P. tobira*). Dense foliage and rapid growth, whether in sun or shade, make this evergreen native of China and Japan a favorite landscape shrub in our region. Its foliage is dark green and leathery or light gray-green rimmed by white in the variegated form. In May pittosporum produces small, sweetly scented blossoms. A hardy, strong grower, it withstands trimming and serves well in assorted landscape plans. Left to its own, it will grow to a large size; dwarf varieties are available for more confined areas.

PITTOSPORUM (Pittosporum tobira)

Plumbago. *See Cape Plumbago*

Poinsettia (*Euphorbia pulcherrima*). Bright red leaves or bracts surround the small, yellow flowers to give the effect of a single, colorful flower in this tropical evergreen plant, which has become a Christmas favorite. The milky sap is poisonous, so "please don't eat the poinsettias." After they bloom, these plants can be cut back and planted in the garden in a sunny, protected spot. Poinsettia's susceptibility to frost makes it appropriate to the milder southern parts of our area only, where it will grow up to ten feet tall.

Pomegranate (*Punica granatum*). Large, showy, orange-red flowers all summer long account for the pomegranate's popularity in the South. A tough, deciduous plant with bright green leaves, it demands full sun. Attaining a height of up to ten feet, it is an excellent specimen plant. Its wide-spreading growth habit should be considered if you are planting it near the house or other structures. Dwarf varieties are available for confined areas. Some pomegranate varieties have large, orange, edible fruit.

Possumhaw (*Ilex decidua*). With brilliant red berries dotting its naked, wide-spreading branches, this holly family member comes into its full glory in winter. A deciduous native with lustrous foliage, it is well adapted to our region's soil and climate conditions. Possumhaw likes sun but will tolerate some shade. It will grow to be twenty-five feet tall. Its fruit attracts birds.

Privet. *See Ligustrum*

Pyracantha, also called **Firethorn** (*P. coccinea*). A vivid, attractive, woody plant, it is deciduous in the North but evergreen

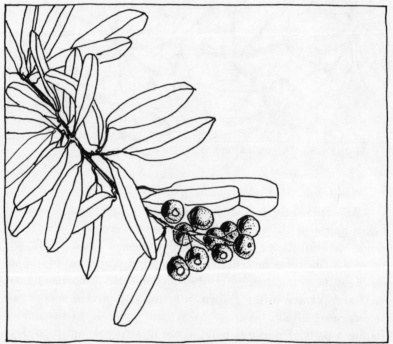

PYRACANTHA OR FIRETHORN (Pyracantha coccinea)

in the South. It is often seen espaliered on walls or fences, showing off bright red berries in the fall and clusters of small, white flowers in the spring. It has small, one-inch long, deep green leaves and a liking for lots of sunshine. Pyracantha will grow to a height over ten feet. Although it is subject to fire blight, it usually thrives in our area.

Quince. *See Japanese Flowering Quince*

Red Hesperaloe, also called **Red Yucca** (*Hesperaloë parviflora*). Bearing a striking resemblance to the true yuccas, this stemless evergreen plant has slender, dark green leaves and long red spikes of conspicuous flowers that bloom throughout the summer. It is slow-growing but wide-reaching and brings the flavor of the Southwest to its setting. Plant it in full sun.

Rosemary. *See ground covers, chapter 6*

Rose of Sharon. *See Shrub Althea*

Roses. *See end of this chapter*

Sage. *See Senisa*

St. John's Wort. *See Gold Flower*

Salt Cedar. *See Kashgar Tamarisk*

Santolina, also called **Cypress Lavender Cotton** (*Santolina chamaecyparissus*). This silver-gray evergreen is a native of southern Europe. It has alternate, woolly leaves about one-half inch long and small, yellow flowers in the summer. A rapid grower eventually reaching 1½ to 2 feet tall, it is often used as a ground cover for poor soils. It is a sun lover. To keep it looking neat requires pruning after the flowering season. *Santolina virens* has narrow, green leaves and can be used for edging.

Senisa, sometimes spelled **Cenizo,** also called **Sage, Texas Silverleaf** (*Leucophyllum frutescens*). This is a local favorite for a number or reasons: silver-gray evergreen foliage with a soft appearance, bell-shaped violet flowers that bloom in high humidity, good adaptation to dry and sandy soil and to either sunny or shady locations. Its attractive, erect shape makes it an excellent choice for medium-sized hedges or as specimens.

Shrub Althea, also called **Rose of Sharon** (*Hibiscus syriacus*). Dating back to colonial times in this country and much earlier abroad, this hardy shrub has three-lobed leaves and colorful, two- to three-inch flowers in rose to purple shades, which appear in late summer. Althea is deciduous, grows from six to twelve feet tall, and can be cut way back in spring to obtain large flowers. This shrub likes sun and can be used as either a specimen or a hedge.

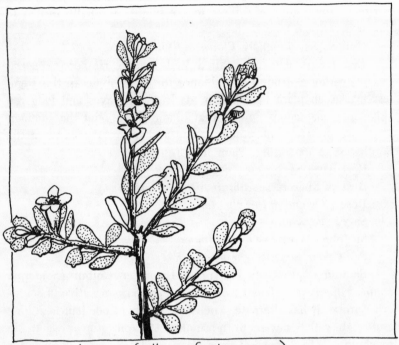

SENISA (Leucophyllum frutescens)

Slender Deutzia (*D. gracilis*). Clusters of white, single flowers cover this low-growing shrub from Japan in early spring. The deciduous leaves are slender, toothed, and 2½ inches long; it needs sunshine for its flowers. Although it is well known and sometimes used as an informal hedge, nurserymen say it is not among the most popular plants, possibly because it needs regular pruning.

Sotol. *See Texas Sotol*

Spirea. *See Bluebeard; Vanhoutte Spirea*

Sumac (*Rhus* spp.). Three of our native sumacs, **Fragrant** (*R. aromatica*), **Flameleaf** (*R. copallina*), and **Evergreen** (*R. sempervirens*), are unusually well suited to the suburban or urban landscape, adding color and texture. With a rangy shape, they reach a height of twelve to twenty-five feet. The flameleaf is the largest and most conspicuous of the three. It transplants easily and provides excellent red color in fall. It is deciduous and sun-loving.

Older, treelike specimens can be found where contractors spared the bulldozer. The evergreen has glossy, leathery leaves that turn a purple-bronze hue in fall. The deciduous *R. aromatica* has a distinctive, delicate, three-lobed leaf that gives off a fragrance when crushed.

Tamarisk. *See Kashgar Tamarisk*

Texas Mountain Laurel, also called **Mescal Bean** (*Sophora secundiflora*). An extravagant profusion of intoxicating flowers and

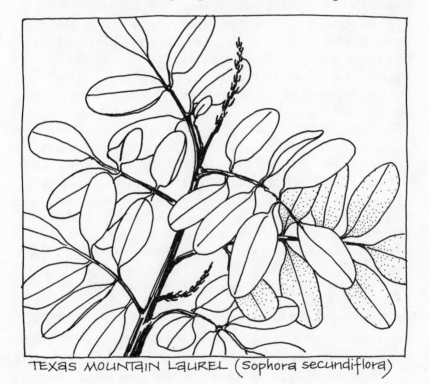

TEXAS MOUNTAIN LAUREL (Sophora secundiflora)

lustrous, dark green leaves make this large shrub or small tree a valuable accent plant. Slowgrowing, but exeptionally suited to Hill Country soils, the native evergreen is available at local nurseries. It blooms best in full sun.

Texas Silverleaf. *See Senisa*

Texas Sotol (*Dasylirion texanum*). Resembling the yuccas, the evergreen tufted lily has leaves that are more slender than yuccas'. Its trunk frequently is located underground, giving the shrub the appearance of a clump of long grass. It grows to three to six feet and requires full sun. In spring, flowers are put out on long spikes.

Thorny Elaeagnus (*E. pungens*). The workhorse of many Southern gardens, this medium-sized evergreen shrub has dappled, gray-green leaves with rusty spots on the underside. An early bloomer, it produces small, fragrant white flowers. It is a good specimen or hedge shrub and will thrive in sun or partial shade.

True Lavender (*Lavandula officinalis*). An old favorite, this evergreen plant is known for its spikes of fragrant lavender flowers that bloom in full sun in early summer. (You can dry the flowers and use them to perfume drawers and garment bags.) It has slender gray leaves about two inches long, grows to over a foot tall, and is sometimes available in a dwarf variety. Propagate by seed, division, and late spring cuttings.

True Myrtle (*Myrtus communis*). From the pages of ancient literature comes this six to nine-foot Mediterranean native with aromatic, glossy evergreen leaves about two inches long and small, creamy white, fragrant flowers, which bloom in spring. The blue-black berries appearing in late summer and fall are an additional attractive feature. The myrtle likes sun and makes a fine hedge. The compact variety is a low, dense plant, very suitable for gardens.

Vanhoutte Spirea (*Spiraea vanhouttei*). The excellent arching habit of this deciduous shrub is one of its best assets and makes it useful as an informal, flowering hedge. Its small white flowers are borne in flat clusters in early spring. It grows about six feet tall in sun or partial shade.

Viburnum (*V.* spp.) This large, versatile, and vigorous family of flowering evergreens well deserves its position as a reliable landscape standard. **Sweet Viburnum** (*V. odoratissimum*) has stout branches and flowers in late spring. In fall, its red fruit turns black. Like most other viburnum, it is seldom bothered by pests of any kind, and it requires little care. Bright, glossy, green leaves offset the fragrant blossoms and the subsequent red berries of the **Sandankwa Viburnum** (*V. suspensum*), making it a very attractive shrub for sunny or partially sunny areas. **Laurestinus Viburnum**

(*V. tinus*) is shade-tolerant and responds well to heavy trimming, making it an excellent hedgerow plant. Viburnum grows to a height of eight to fifteen feet.

Vitex (*V. agnus-castus*). Preferring dry, sunny conditions, this long-blooming native produces great spikes of fragrant blue-violet flowers, often used in sachet. Its toothed, lance-shaped leaflets appear in groups of five or more. The vitex has many trunks and grows to twenty feet. It makes either a good accent or a good border.

Yaupon (*Ilex vomitoria*). Small (twenty-foot maximum height) and slender with a rugged, often crooked gray trunk to give it character, this native evergreen holly is a perfect specimen plant. Bright red berries are borne on the female in winter, and the leaves are small and elliptical. The yaupon is available at nurseries, but it often grows wild as a companion to oak in Central Texas. Its curious species name refers to its former medicinal use. The dwarf yaupon thrives in shade or sun. Dense and compact, it is effective as a border or specimen shrub, or it can be grown as an impenetrable hedge, tolerant of heavy trimming.

Yew. *See Japanese Yew*

Yucca (*Y.* spp.). These natives of the American Southwest are characterized by their long, thick, evergreen, daggerlike leaves. Singular in appearance, yuccas do equally well as accent plants grouped with other shrubs or as specimen shrubs in succulent gardens. The **Aloe Yucca** (*Y. aloifolia*) grows to 10 feet. Showy white flowers on 1- to 1½-foot spikes appear in late spring or early summer. The **Twistleaf Yucca** (*Y. rupicola*) is a small, low-growing plant, sending up tall spikes of greenish white flowers late in spring. The **Spanish Dagger** (*Y. treculeara*) is a spectacular tree of 5 to 25 feet, with a simple or branched trunk. Extravagant flowers on a 1- to 4-foot spike appear in spring. Its distinctive and exotic appearance makes it a popular specimen plant. *See also Red Hesperaloe.*

Roses

It is probably the combination of the flower form, the fragrance, and the beautiful color that have earned the rose the title of "queen of flowers." This splendid member of the plant kingdom (botanically classified as a shrub) has been enticing gardeners and occupying a privileged spot in the landscape since time immemorial. Their unique status, as well as the abundance of varieties and special care requirements, have entitled roses to a separate section in this book.

Although there are many (fifty to seventy-five in America) so-called true rose species, the varieties that are most popular in our gardens today are the results of mutation and hybridization from primitive native roses. These favorites are the hybrid tea roses, floribundas, grandifloras, climbing roses, and miniature roses.

Hybrid teas are without doubt the most popular roses in gardens and greenhouses. They come in practically every color you might want, and many are also fragrant. Hybrid teas are bushy and

HYBRID TEA ROSE

have large, single flowers or small clusters with either single blooms (one row of petals) or double blooms (many rows). In our climate they bloom in spring and fall and intermittently in summer. They are hardy but require care to prevent disease and insect damage.

The following roses have received high ratings from the American Rose Society[1] and the South Central District of the Society.

Chicago Peace (pink blend), Chrysler Imperial (dark red), First Prize (pink blend), Garden Party (white), Granada (red blend), Mister Lincoln (dark red), Peace (yellow blend), Royal Highness (light pink), Swarthmore (pink blend), and Tropicana (orange-red). Other, newer varieties that are claiming attention in our area are: Alabama (pink blend), Double Delight (red blend), Pristine (white), and Honor (white), the 1980 "rose of the year."

Floribundas. Although they generally produce smaller flowers than the hybrid teas, the floribundas feature clusters of blossoms and color in the garden beginning in the spring and on through late fall for a longer period of time than hybrid tea roses. They are also apt to be more hardy and disease-resistant.

Listed below are some of the varieties popular in Central Texas.

Angel Face (mauve), Europeana (dark red), Fire King (orange-red), Gene Boerner (medium pink), Ginger (orange-red), First Prize (pink blend), Handel (red blend), Lawrence Pink Rosette (pink), Sarabande (orange-red), and Vogue (pink blend.

Grandifloras. A cross between the hybrid tea and the floribunda, the grandiflora produces large blooms, usually one per stem, but in the formation of a cluster. They are about as hardy as hybrid teas.

Some recommended varieties are listed here.

Aquarius (pink blend), Camelot (medium pink), Granada (red blend), Golden Girl (medium yellow), Montezuma (orange-red), Mount Shasta (white), Pink Parfait (pink blend),

[1]American Rose Society, Box 30,000, Shreveport, Louisiana 71130

Queen Elizabeth (medium pink), Sonia (pink blend), and Sundowner (apricot blend).

Climbing Roses. Although roses have no special climbing equipment, some varieties produce long shoots or canes that can be trained over fences and trellises. Climbing roses vary on many characteristics, including length of blooming period and size of flowers.

When choosing for your garden, you might want to consider the following varieties.

America (orange-red), Casa Blanca (white), Don Juan (dark red), First Prize (pink blend), Handel (red blend), Lawrence Johnston (medium yellow), and Royal Sunset (apricot blend).

Miniature Roses. The delicate buds, stems, and foliage of miniature roses have made them very popular with certain rose enthusiasts. They come in a great variety of colors, grow from three inches to a foot tall, and, for continuous blooming, can be grown indoors as potted plants and then put outside when warm weather arrives.

Here are a group of popular miniature roses.

Beauty Secret (medium red), Chipper (light pink), Cinderella (white), Judy Fischer (medium pink), Magic Carrousel (red blend), Mary Marshall (orange-pink), Over-the-Rainbow (red blend), Scarlet Gem (orange-red), Starina (orange-red), and Toy Clown (red blend).

Care of Roses

Since roses require special treatment and care, we need to say a few words about the routine required to keep them healthy and beautiful.

Bare-root roses should be planted in winter from late November through February. Container roses can be planted any time, but spring and fall are preferable. Roses like slight acidity—a pH of 6.0 to 6.5—so chances are you will have to add sulphur and copperas as well as a large amount of humus to the soil. However, if you don't have deep, black soil for roses, you should dig out a bed about fifteen inches deep and fill it with new soil, raising the bed about six inches above the soil level to facilitate drainage. A local rosarian suggests substituting for the original soil a mixture of one-third coarse sand, one-third black soil, and one-third peat moss or compost. This bed should be prepared at least a week before planting time.

Roses should be planted about eight to ten inches deep and two feet apart. Follow the general rules for planting (see chapter 7). Water well and mound the soil around the bush to protect it from damaging winter winds. Our rosarian mulches in the spring with pine needles (he goes to Bastrop for his). You can also use pine bark, leaves, or compost to help retain moisture and control weeds.

Roses should be fed about every six weeks beginning in spring and ending in September, for a total of four feedings. If you're growing show roses you may feed as often as every two weeks. Use a good commercial rose fertilizer. Remember to water roses thoroughly, at least once a week and as often as two times a week during extremely hot, dry weather.

The most troublesome part of raising roses comes under the heading of pest and disease control. Someone at your garden center can recommend fungicides and insecticides to solve the problem. If you wish to follow the regimen of one local rosarian, here it is: beginning in spring, and again in fall, spray once a week for black spot and mildew with one-half-strength benomyl and one-half-strength Maneb. Beginning in April use diazinon once a week for chewing insects and malathion for thrips. This expert adds one teaspoon of vinegar to a gallon of water to increase the effectiveness of the malathion; he also adds one teaspoon of a liquid detergent to his insecticide and fungicide mixes. This helps retain the mixture on the leaves.

Rose bushes are pruned to produce more and better blossoms, and for that reason their pruning needs are more demanding than those of other shrubs. Pruning begins with cutting back dead and diseased canes to the live wood and removing suckers coming up from the roots. Next, prune to shape. The rigid rose-pruning orthodoxy of years ago has been replaced by greater latitude in letting the gardener exercise his or her judgment. Roses can be pruned high, medium, or low. While there are many opinions on what the optimal cut is, it is safe to remove one-third to one-half of the previous year's growth. The cane should be cut about a quarter-inch above an outward pointing bud at a thirty-degree angle. When you direct the growth outward, the plant will have good sunshine and air circulation.

Hybrid teas, floribundas, and grandifloras should be pruned in the spring. Large-flowered climbers are also pruned lightly in the spring. Climbers that bloom only in the spring should be pruned after they blossom.

If flowers are cut, late-summer pruning often is unnecessary. Otherwise, it is advisable to prune in a similar manner, although somewhat less severely.

Remember always to make your cut with a sharp tool. Ragged cuts may fail to heal, making them vulnerable to insect and disease invasion.

Roses sold in containers seldom need pruning when transplanted to their spot in the garden. Most nurserymen, thinking of sales, have kept them looking their best. However, roses purchased in the bare-root state need extra care to assure a good start and healthy growth. The rose should be soaked overnight in water, and the dead or damaged roots removed. After the bush has been properly planted, the canes should be cut back to six or eight inches to compensate for the root loss.

Despite the demanding regimen, most gardeners are tempted to try roses at one time or another. And as one knowledgeable rosarian said to us: "No flowering plant is as gratifying. In our area you can actually have roses in bloom for nine months of the year." For many that's reason enough to grow the "queen of flowers."

10

Vines and Climbers

Along the ground from root to root; or climbing
high with random maze. . . .
                    Edith Holden, *The Country Diary of an*
                    Edwardian Lady

DON'T overlook the vines and other climbers. They can play an
important part in your landscaping plans. Their climbing or trailing growth habits can give a rich appearance to your yard by con-
cealing unsightly features such as rocks, privacy fences, or tool-
sheds and work areas. Vines also can enhance, by either softening
or emphasizing, gateways and doorways. They can turn stark wood,
masonry, and even chain link fencing into a green hanging blanket.
A few vines that are noted for their tenacious growth also serve
well as ground covers in areas where there is little or no foot traffic; the ivies and Asiatic jasmine are good examples of this category. Many vines have spectacular blossoms and/or colorful fruit.
Vines come in both evergreen and deciduous varieties.

Climbing is achieved by three basic methods: twining, attaching by tendrils or leaf stalks, or clinging fast to a surface with small
disks or rootlike projections. Vines that twine and attach themselves
by means of tendrils and leaf stalks require wire or a trellis or other
lattice work for support. Clingers need only a surface or tree trunk
to which to attach themselves. Knowledge of how vines grow is
essential for selecting the proper plant for a given situation. For
instance, you would not want to choose a twining vine to cover a
stone wall since it could not hold.

When you plant, place the vine at least one foot from the surface it is intended to cover. Remember, too, that soil near building
foundations, a popular location for vines and climbers, often is im-
poverished and requires more enrichment with organic matter and

more frequent watering than other areas. As you would for any plant, make a generous-sized hole to allow roots to spread freely. Vines may be fertilized annually in early spring with a balanced fertilizer; however, if overgrowth threatens, you may want to withhold the fertilizer.

Most people tend to neglect pruning their vines until the situation is out of control. While most vines will survive severe treatment with the pruning shears, the gardener who regularly removes suckers, dead sections, and stems that have gone awry will enjoy a neater appearance. Vines that fall or are blown from their support require special attention, as the old growth will not reattach itself. In these cases, plants should be cut back drastically and the new growth supported by means of ties or hooks until the vine has reestablished itself.

Wisteria, valued most for its rich blossoms, should have its new growth cut back to spurs of two buds apiece in the fall to maximize flowering the following spring. If wisteria has been neglected over a long period of time, root pruning may be necessary to stimulate blossoming.

Listed below are desirable vines and climbers, both natives and introduced ornamentals, that are well adapted to the Central Texas environment.

A Checklist of Popular Vines and Climbers

Balsam Gourd (*Ibervillea lindheimeri*). A member of the cucumber family, this native vine produces oval leaves and a striped blossom of yellow and pale green. Its real glory, however, is the large (one- to two-inch) orange-red fruit. Country folk like to plant this deciduous vine along barbed-wire fences. In the wild it prefers full sun in open woods and thickets. It climbs by tendrils.

Bougainvillea (*B.* spp.). Producing abundant blossoms of intense shades of pink, red, orange, yellow, or purple, this tropical twining vine requires a sunny and sheltered location. While bougainvillea will withstand mild winters in south-central Texas, north of Austin it is best to plant this deciduous vine in pots to be brought in to winter. Plant with care, as the root system is delicate, and mulch for winter protection. Applications of a 10-5-10 fertilizer in spring and again in summer will guarantee a long period of blossoms. While it grows from sixty to a hundred feet in tropical environments, we can expect it to reach a length of twenty to thirty feet in Central Texas. Pruning keeps the vine vigorous. New plants can be started from softwood cuttings taken in late spring or early summer.

Chinese Wisteria (*W. sinensis*). This prime ornamental vine rapidly climbs by twining to twenty-five feet. Large clusters of

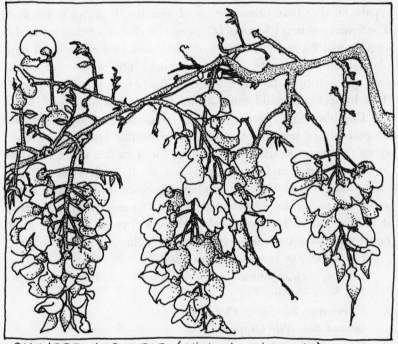

CHINESE WISTERIa (Wisteria sinensis)

fragrant, sun-loving flowers in violet-blue appear before the leaves in spring. It climbs from left to right and has light green foliage with seven to thirteen leaflets. It can be propagated asexually from plants that flower early. In this area, it is sometimes grafted so that it grows in tree form.

Clematis (*C.* spp.). Several native species of this delicately branching deciduous genus bear beautiful, conspicuous flowers, making them very desirable for cultivation. Their leaves are compound. All species flower best when planted in full sun. They grow to be several yards long. The **Old Man's Beard** (*C. drummondii*) produces a white blossom with numerous, very long stamens, March through September. It is partial to sun and well-drained soil. In the wild, the **Scarlet Clematis** (*C. texensis*) is most at home on the Edwards Plateau, preferring limestone outcroppings or rich soil. The striking red, bell-shaped flower is formed by four leathery sepals. Smaller than other species of clematis, it grows to ten feet. The **Sweet-autumn Clematis** (*C. paniculata*) was introduced in this country in 1864 and has flourished ever since. One of the most popular fall-blooming vines, it bears fragrant white blossoms of a delicate appearance. Attaining a length of thirty feet, this vine attaches itself by leaf stalks and can withstand heavy pruning.

Climbing Fig (*Ficus pumila*). Its dense growing habit and adaptability to semishade conditions make this fast-growing evergreen vine very popular for use on southern garden walls. A native to China, Japan, and Australia, it has small rootlets for clinging and grows to sixty feet. Older plants produce inedible figs. It has small but numerous oval-shaped leaves. It needs pruning to keep it healthy and attractive. Harsh winters will cause it to die back, but it will grow back from its roots the following spring.

Coralvine. *See Mountain Rose Coralvine*

Creeper. *See Japanese Creeper; Trumpetvine; Virginia Creeper*

Fig. *See Climbing Fig*

Fleecevine. *See Silver Fleecevine*

Grapes. *See Wild Grapes*

Honeysuckle (*Lonicera* spp.). Climbing vine or sprawling ground cover, the honeysuckle is one of our most versatile plants. If the weather cooperates (gives us enough moisture), honeysuckle fills the air with its familiar sweet fragrance several times a year. It is little wonder that so many find a place for this vine in their gardens. **Purple Japanese Honeysuckle** (*L. japonica* var. *chinensis*) and **Hall's Japanese Honeysuckle** (*L. japonica* var. *halliana*) are two common species in our area. Both are evergreen and fast-growing, preferring full to partial sun. Flowers usually appear from late spring through early summer. New blossoms of Hall's are white, gradually fading to a yellowing ivory shade as they age. Both varieties grow to thirty feet by twining. They may be left to sprawl over banks or trained to trellises. The beauty of the evergreen **Trumpet Honeysuckle** (*L. sempervirens*) is more than adequate compensation for its lack of scent. The long (1½- to 2-inch) tubular blossoms are orange or scarlet with yellow interiors, and the fruit is a favorite among cardinals and purple finches. Climbing rapidly up to fifty feet, the trumpet honeysuckle blooms best when planted in full sun.

Ivy (*Hedera* spp.). Clinging to walls, holding onto trees, or just filling in the shady spots, the ivies are among our most useful plants. Two evergreen species popular in our area are the **Algerian Ivy** (*H. canariensis*) and the **English Ivy** (*H. helix*). The Algerian ivy has large, glossy leaves and is resistant to heat and drought. A rapid grower, it is an excellent plant for erosion control. Although its leaves are smaller and it grows more slowly, the English ivy is extremely hardy, and given rich, moist soil it will do better in full sun than the Algerian ivy. Both ivies grow to around forty feet. Occasionally they produce small, inconspicuous flowers and fruits, but these are of little interest or value.

Ivy Treebine (*Cissus incisa*). This woody vine has attractive, deeply incised leaves, which produce an unpleasant odor when crushed. Clusters of small, greenish flowers are produced in summer, followed by small, shiny black inedible fruit. This deciduous native does well in shade as well as full sun. Growing rapidly by means of tendrils, it will utilimately reach up to thirty feet.

Japanese Creeper, also called **Boston Ivy** (*Parthenocissus tricuspidata*). Widely used in landscape plantings, this agile, fast-growing climber may get to sixty feet by attaching rootlike holdfasts to its means of support. It takes sun to partial shade. It is deciduous and has alternate, mostly three-lobed leaves, which may be eight inches wide. The cuttings root readily; layers found near older plants and suckers can also be used.

Jasmine. The five commonly used vines referred to as jasmine or jessamine do not even share the same genus name. All are very well suited to our area, produce fragrant flowers, and perform well in many roles. **Star Jasmine** (*Trachelospermum jasminoides*) has been a staple in southern gardens so long that it is often affectionately called **Confederate Jasmine**. Its dark, shiny, evergreen leaves provide an excellent background for the pure white flowers. Growing well in partial shade as well as in full sun, it provides a thick covering rapidly and is used as widely as a ground covering as it is a climber. **Asiatic Jasmine** (*Trachelospermum asiaticum*) is another evergreen vine that serves well in the dual role of ground

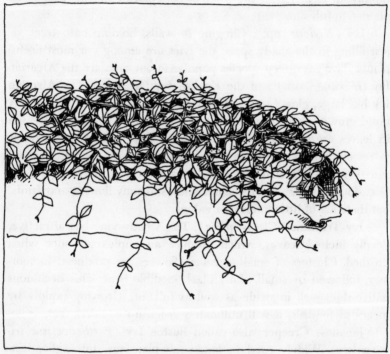

JASMINE, ASIATIC (Trachelospermum asiaticum)

cover or climber. Its flowers and leaves are taller than those of the star jasmine. Sun-loving, moderately fast-growing, and drought-resistant, it is useful along steep banks. The flowers are yellowish white, and the new leaves bear a bronze cast. Both *Trachelospermum* species are twiners. The long, willowy branches of

Primrose Jasmine (*Jasminum mesnyi*) bear large, golden flowers in late winter or early spring. Its mounding habit gives it more the appearance of a shrub than of a vine. It is suited equally well as a specimen or in groups as a hedgerow. Its semi-evergreen foliage is composed of thick, shiny leaves. Blooming best in full sun, it will attain a height of five to seven feet and will spread to four to five feet. Similar in appearance and habit is the **Italian Jasmine** (*Jasminum humile*). Its flowers are smaller and bloom later in the season. The evergreen foliage has three to seven dark green leaflets. It takes full sun to partial shade. The **Carolina Jessamine** (*Gelsemium sempervirens*) is an attractive evergreen vine that produces delicate yellow flowers early in the season if it gets full sun. A native of the Carolinas, it is a popular twining vine in Central Texas landscape designs, where it climbs ten to twenty feet at a moderate rate. It has shiny, oblong leaves.

Lady Banksia Rose (*Rosa banksiae*). These beautiful, tender Chinese roses are often seen climbing fifteen to forty feet up a wall or tree in our gardens. Left on its own, this vine will rapidly assume a wild appearance; happily, it responds well to pruning and training. The *lutea* variety is double yellow and has flowers about one inch wide. *Alba-plena* variety has double white flowers, which are slightly fragrant. This deciduous, twining rose blooms best in full sun to partial shade.

Mountain Rose Coralvine, also called **Queen's Wreath** (*Antigonon leptopus*). Known in Mexico as the chain-of-love vine, this deciduous native displays series of small, pink, heart-shaped blossoms from late summer to early fall. The leaves too are heart shaped. Attaching itself by tendrils, the coralvine will grow rapidly to forty feet. It requires full sun to partial shade.

Passionflower (*Passiflora caerulea*). A Brazilian native that uses tendrils to climb rapidly up to twenty feet in our warm Southern gardens, it produces large-lobed leaves and attractive blue or purple to white flowers, four inches across, when planted in full sun. Although susceptible to frost, it will grow back in the spring.

Peppervine (*Ampelopsis arborea*). This slender, rapid climber grows best in rich, moist soil and shade. Small flowers in June through July develop into shiny, black, inedible fruit in fall. The dark green, deciduous leaflets are deeply incised, giving the vine a delicate appearance. New leaves may have a reddish bronze cast. This vine climbs by tendrils.

Rose. *See Lady Banksia Rose*

Silver Fleecevine, also called **Silverlace Vine** (*Polygonum aubertii*). This good-looking, vigorous vine may twine twenty to thirty feet in one season. Its small, white or greenish white flowers bloom in dense clusters during late summer. The deciduous vine does well in full sun or partial shade. It looks good on a chain link fence, which it will take over in no time. It will withstand severe pruning.

Treebine. *See Ivy Treebine*

Trumpetcreeper. *See Trumpetvine*

Trumpetvine, also called **Trumpetcreeper** (*Campsis radicans*). A native of the southeastern United States, this rapid-growing clinging vine is easily recognized by the orange to scarlet, trumpet-shaped flowers that bloom in summer, most profusely in full sun, and are well loved by hummingbirds. Trumpetvine's deciduous leaves are compound and have nine to eleven leaflets. It climbs to twenty or thirty feet and becomes very heavy; if it does not have support, it may break away from the walls on which it grows.

Virginia Creeper (*Parthenocissus quinquefolia*). Growing wild throughout much of the United States, this deciduous creeper no doubt owes its popularity as a cultivated vine to the very attractive palmately compound leaves, which turn scarlet in autumn. In an area noticeably lacking red in its fall color scheme, the Virginia creeper is a welcome addition. Its small, blue berries are cherished by birds. It does equally well clinging to trees, walls, and fences or trailing on the ground, and it tolerates full sun to partial shade.

Wild Grapes (*Vitis* spp.). Several species of native grapes make attractive vines and provide good fruit for preserves or wild-life food. The broad, often toothed, deciduous leaves are of a pleasing shape, and their lush growth lends a Southern look to the landscape. **Winter Grape** (*V. berlandieri*), **Mustang Grape** (*V. candicans*), and **Summer Grape** (*V. aestivalis*) are among the most

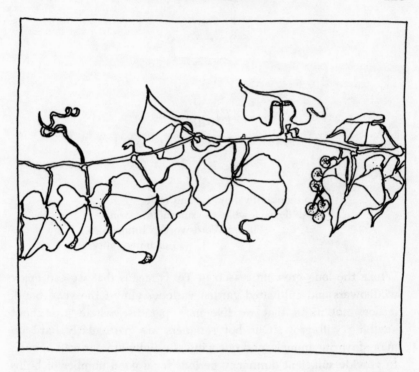

commonly found in the area. Rapid growers (to forty feet), they are most productive in full sun to partial shade. Cuttings and layering are successful methods for propagating grapes. Any transplanting of grape vines should be done in January through February. All grapes climb by tendrils.

Wisteria. *See Chinese Wisteria*

11

Flowers

In a thousand valleys far and wide,
Fresh flowers; while the sun shines warm. . . .
William Wordsworth, "Intimations
of Immortality"

WHILE the long growing season in Texas means that we can enjoy wildflowers and cultivated garden varieties almost the year-round, it does not mean that we live in a paradise where just about anything will grow. Our hot summers are particularly hard on many favorite annuals, and our winters usually are not cold enough to provide sufficient dormancy periods for a good number of bulbs and perennials. Selecting varieties that are well adapted to our climate is the surest way to successful flower gardening.

The best flower beds are well planned. Become familiar with the different available species through magazines, catalogs, and, best of all, visits to area garden centers, but don't buy on the first trip out. Before purchasing or planting a single flower, plan your flower garden on graph paper. Keeping the plan to scale will help you calculate the number of plants and the amount of fertilizer you will need. We recommend that you use crayons or colored markers when drawing up the plan. This way you will get an idea of the overall effect of your color scheme. Sometimes it's best to have the surprises show up on paper first.

Your first consideration in planning a flower bed is location. Many flowers bloom best if they receive five to six hours of sun. In our climate, the cooler morning sun is preferable but not essential, especially for shallow-rooted annuals. Try to place your beds so that they do not interfere with your other garden chores. Many small beds scattered about the yard will make mowing, edging, and watering more difficult and time-consuming.

Second, think about the amount of time and care you wish to devote to garden work. While extra attention will be rewarded, an attractive flower bed can be simple and carefree. Flowers planted in pots provide color for small areas and reduce work. A trowel will do the job of the garden hoe and spade, a watering can replaces miles of hose, and smaller amounts of fertilizer and pesticides are needed. It is important to remember that potted plants require smaller applications of fertilizer at slightly more frequent intervals. Also, containers must provide for drainage, and watering chores cannot be neglected.

Demanding more work and attention in the initial preparation, perennials, once established, go on for years with a little weeding, one or two annual applications of fertilizer, and division of overgrown plants every three to five years. Annuals must be planted each year and watered and fertilized more frequently. While some gardeners welcome the opportunity to start anew each year, others prefer to watch an established bed mature through the years. Because interest in a garden is provided by an assortment of color, texture, shape, and size, we prefer flower beds that contain both annuals and perennials. Years ago, when the guiding philosophy for flower gardens was more formal, it was fashionable to have a yellow bed, a blue bed, and so forth. Today rules are less rigid, and creativity is encouraged; gardeners are free to make their own choices.

Be sure to note on your plan spacing requirements and flower heights. Taller flowers, while they should not necessarily be relegated to the back row, must not be allowed to interfere with the light requirements of smaller plants or to block your view of them. Gardening chores will be easier if you group together plants with similar watering needs.

Finally, a flower garden with little in bloom does not give much pleasure, and flower beds that are neglected because nothing is blooming are quickly invaded by weeds and grass. Choose your flowers to provide seasonal color, and not only will you prolong your enjoyment but you will be practicing good gardening, too.

Annuals

Since their entire lives span only one season, annuals tirelessly produce an abundance of flowers in an effort to make seed and ensure another generation. This and the joy of planting a seed and watching it grow are among the reasons so many people grow annuals.

ANNUALS: PORTULACA, MARIGOLD, PETUNIA

Although these flowers vary widely in hardiness, our heat is a challenge to a number of them. Not only does the summer sun increase the evaporation rate for the tender-leaved plants; it also raises the soil temperature intolerably for shallow root systems. For that reason we have recommended varieties that are suitable for Central Texas.

Annuals are grown from seed or purchased as bedding plants from area nurseries. Before visiting a nursery for your selections, plan ahead and think about what would look best in your garden and how you want to use annuals—in a bed, as a border, or to accent certain areas. Next consider the plants' light, soil, and spacing needs and whether you can meet them. While general rules are broken as quickly in gardening as anywhere else, one can say that most annuals like sun, moisture, and good drainage. With selections improving each year, we find it difficult to restrain ourselves from purchasing one of each kind. However, one petunia, one marigold, and one cosmos just won't do very much for your garden. Mass plantings are far more effective.

If you are creating a flower bed for the first time, loosen the soil in the fall and add organic matter. Then in the spring, cultivate again and, before planting, add more organic matter and the proper amount of 5-10-5 fertilizer for the size of your garden. Seeds sometimes fail to germinate if the soil has hardened over them. If you are planting seed directly in the ground, you can avoid this problem by lining one- to two-inch furrows with vermiculite. Water the vermiculite, plant the seed, cover with more vermiculite, and water again. Keep the soil moist until the seedlings appear.

While the average depth for annuals (except for very fine seed, which often is not covered at all) is one-eighth to one-quarter inch, it is frequently recommended to double this figure when sowing seeds in summer. Flowers planted in spring need to feel the sun's warmth, but those planted during the summer need extra protection from the burning heat.

If you are starting annuals in flats indoors (see propagation, chapter 3), do not start earlier than eight weeks before the frost-free date. Plants started earlier will be ready to go outdoors long before the weather is ready for them. Overstaying their welcome in the flat will result in long, spindly, weak seedlings. Most annuals have small root systems and can be transplanted easily. When transplanting container-grown plants or seedlings from flats, be sure to plant them in holes large enough to allow the entire root system to extend downward.

Watering, fertilizing, and pest control are the remaining maintenance procedures. As many annuals are susceptible to mildew, watering by soaker hose is better than using an overhead sprinkler.

When the soil is dry, water deeply, at a depth of one to two inches. Always water gently. Mulching will conserve moisture, discourage weeds, and add to the attractiveness of the flower bed. Fertilize with a balanced fertilizer (5-10-5) every four to eight weeks. Avoid getting fertilizer on the foliage, and water thoroughly afterward.

When plants are two to four inches tall, they may be "pinched back" by removing the uppermost leaves. This practice encourages bushier growth and more blossoms. If you wish to produce larger, single blossoms, "disbud," or remove all but the terminal bud. The blooming season is prolonged by removing spent blossoms before the plant goes into seed production.

Annuals

Name	Height (inches)	Color	Exposure	Planting Time	Blooming Time	Comments
Ageratum (*A.* spp.)	6–20	blue, pink, white	sun to partial shade	bedding plants available March–April	summer–fall	Good border plant. Space 6 to 9 inches apart.
Alyssum (*Lobularia maritima*)	4–8	white to violet	sun	after frost-free date	summer–fall	Remove old blossoms to prolong blooming. Will withstand frost. Space 6 to 8 inches apart.
Amaranthus, also called **Joseph's Coat** (*A. tricolor*)	36	bronze, green, yellow tones	sun	after frost-free date	summer–fall	Brilliantly variegated foliage. Likes dry soil. Space 18 to 36 inches apart. Dwarf forms from 4 to 8 inches are also available; plant these 6 to 12 inches apart.
Black-eyed Susan (*Thunbergia alata*)	vine, 72	yellow, brown center	sun to partial shade	after frost-free date	all summer	Good ground cover or trellis climber. Plant 3 inches away from support.

Name	Height (inches)	Color	Exposure	Planting Time	Blooming Time	Comments
Calendula, also called Pot Marigold (*C. officinalis*)	10–24	yellow-white	sun to partial shade	October–December in Central Texas; February–April in North Central Texas	winter–spring	Prefers cool weather. Rarely blooms after May. Space 12 to 15 inches apart.
Candle Tree, also called Emperor's Candlestick (*Cassia alata*)	72	yellow	sun	container-grown plants in spring	summer	Growing in popularity, this annual owes much of its grandeur to its enormous size. Large spikes of yellow blossoms are surrounded by handsome compound leaves. Before you plant, make sure you have adequate space and set plants 3 to 4 feet apart.
Candytuft (*Iberis* spp.)	6–16	white and	sun to partial	early spring–late fall	January–April	Easy to grow, fine for cutting. Smaller variety

		many colors	shade			makes an excellent border plant. Plant at 6- to 9-inch intervals.
Cape Marigold (*Dimorphotheca* spp.)	12	white, salmon, rose, yellow	sun	after frost-free date	summer–fall	Very long growing season. Likes hot, dry areas. Space 10 inches apart.
Chinese Forget-Me-not (*Cynoglossum amabile*)	24	blue	sun to partial shade	October–December	spring	Prefers dry soil. Space 12 inches apart.
Cleome, also called **Spider Flower** (*Cleome* spp.)	36–48	pink, white	sun	after frost-free date	summer–fall	Prefers hot, dry location. Almost any soil will do. Space at 24-inch intervals.
Cockscomb (*Celosia*)	6–24	red, pink, orange	sun	after frost-free date	summer–fall	Likes dry soil. Flowers are extremely long-lasting. Space 9 to 12 inches apart.
Coleus (*C. blumei*)	8–24	red, green, pink, white	sun or partial shade	after frost-free date	summer–fall	Although the coleus does produce a flower, it is best loved for its spectacularly variegated foliage from

Name	Height (inches)	Color	Exposure	Planting Time	Blooming Time	Comments
						late spring through the fall. Leaf color will be more vivid if the plants are not overfertilized. Plant at 8- to 10-inch intervals.
Copper Plant (*Acalypha wilkesiana*)	36	copper	sun	after frost-free date	summer–fall	Brilliant foliage. Needs plenty of fertilizer. Heat-tolerant. Space 18 to 24 inches apart.
Cornflower, also called **Bachelor's Button** (*Centaurea cyanus*)	12–36	white, blue, red, pink	sun	October–January	February–April	Prolific, requiring little care. Space at 12-inch intervals.
Cosmos (*C.* spp.)	24–30	white, pink, red,	sun	after frost-free date	summer–fall	Excellent choice for our location. Has very long blooming season. Don't

		yellow, and orange				overfertilize. Transplants easily. Plant 12 incnes apart.
Dusty Miller (*Centaurea gymnocarpa*)	12	yellow	sun	after frost-free date	summer	Unusual white foliage. Here is another example of a flower appreciated more for its interesting foliage than for the small yellow flower it produces in summer. The deep-lobed, light gray leaves add variety to any flower bed. Space at twelve-inch intervals.
Forget-Me-Not (*Myosotis spp.*)	9–12	mostly blue, some white, pink	partial shade	spring–summer	late winter–spring	Good cutting flowers. Space at 6- to 8-inch intervals.
Gaillardia (*G. spp.*)	18	orange, yellow	sun	after frost-free date	summer–fall	Particularly well suited to our area. Good cut flowers. Plant at 8-inch intervals.

Name	Height (inches)	Color	Exposure	Planting Time	Blooming Time	Comments
Garden Balsam (*Impatiens balsamina*)	6–12	white, pink, red, and multi-colored	partial shade	after frost-free date	all summer	A nice border plant, garden balsam is easy to propagate from cuttings. Water frequently. Space 15 inches apart.
Geranium (*Pelargonium* spp.)	12–24	white, pink, red	full sun at least half a day, preferably morning	after frost-free date	spring and again in fall	In frost-free areas geraniums are perennials, attaining a height of 4 to 5 feet. Because they require five months from seed to flower, it is wisest to purchase potted plants and plant in medium rich soil. Space 12 inches apart.
Godetia (*G.* spp.)	10–30	white, pink, lilac	sun to partial shade	October–December	spring	Good cut flowers. Will not tolerate extreme summer heat. Plant 6 to 12 inches apart.

Name	Height (inches)	Color	Light	Planting	Blooming	Comments
Gypsophila, also called **Baby's Breath** (*G. elegans*)	12–18	white, pink, rose	sun	after frost-free date	late spring	Likes alkaline soil not too rich in nutrients. Good cut flowers. Plant 8 to 12 inches apart.
Impatiens (*I. wallerana*)	6–15	pink, red, white, purple	shade	after frost-free date	June–October	One of the few annuals to prefer shade. Encourage more blossoms and bushier growth by pinching back the main stem; detached portions may be rooted to produce more plants. Space 12 inches apart.
Larkspur (*Delphinium ajacis*)	30–36	blue, rose, purple, white	sun to partial	October–December	May–July	Good cut flower. Susceptible to mildew and aphids. Seeds need cool weather to germinate. Plant 8 to 15 inches apart.
Linaria, also called Toadflax (*L. maroccana*)	15–18	white and colors	sun	October–December	early spring	Prefers cool weather. Provides long-lasting cut flowers. Plant at 6-inch intervals.

Name	Height (inches)	Color	Exposure	Planting Time	Blooming Time	Comments
Marigold (*Tagetes* spp.)	6–36	yellow, orange, rust	partial shade	after frost-free date	late spring–fall	One of America's favorite annuals, probably because it almost never fails. Reputed to discourage nematodes, making it an ideal companion for tomato plants. Plant at 6- to 18-inch intervals.
Morning Glory (*Ipomoea purpurea*)	Trailing vine up to 72	white, blue	sun	after frost-free date	late spring–summer	Cheerful, profuse blossoms are well accented when supported by fence or trellis. Does not transplant well. Plant 8 to 12 inches apart.
Nasturtium (*Tropaeolum* spp.)	12–48	yellow, orange, mahogany	partial shade	October–December in Central Texas; February–April in North Central Texas	spring	Will not bloom in too rich soil. Takes neglect well. Requires good drainage. Does not transplant well. Plant 6 to 12 inches apart.

Name	Height (in.)	Color	Exposure	Planting time	Bloom time	Notes
Nierembergia (*N. caerulea*)	6	blue-violet	sun to partial shade	January–February	April–May, again in September	This biennial will bloom the second spring if winter is mild. Plant 6 to 8 inches apart.
Pansy (*Viola tricolor var. hortensis*)	8	shades of red, purple, blue, yellow, white	sun to partial shade	October–December	November–May	Likes soil rich in humus. Fertilize every three to four weeks. Keep moist. Picking faded flowers will extend blooming season. Difficult to start from seed; buy potted plants. Space 10 to 12 inches apart.
Periwinkle, also called Madagascar Vinca (*Vinca rosea*)	10–18	white, pink, lavender	sun	after frost-free date	summer–fall	Loving heat, blooms all summer long in Central Texas. The attractive foliage is dark green with light-colored veins. Space 8 to 10 inches apart.
Petunia (*P. spp.*)	6–12	red, blue, pink,	sun	after frost-free date	May–summer	New hybrids are introduced constantly. Difficulty in raising from seed makes

Name	Height (inches)	Color	Exposure	Planting Time	Blooming Time	Comments
		purple, orange, white, mixed				the purchase of bedding plants a bargain. Hybrids cannot be grown successfully two years in a row. Rotate with another crop. Space 8 to 12 inches apart.
Phlox (*P. drummondii*)	15–18	white and many shades of yellow pink, lavender, red	sun	after frost-free date	summer	Heat-tolerant. Good cut flower. Space 6 to 10 inches apart.
Pink (*Dianthus chinensis*)	6–12	white, red, pink, yellow, mixtures	sun	October–December in Central Texas; February–April in North Central Texas	spring–summer	Well disposed toward alkaline soils. Vivid colors. Space at 6- to 10-inch intervals.

Name	Height (inches)	Color	Light	When to plant	Bloom	Remarks
Poppy, California (*Eschscholtzia californica*)	12–15	scarlet, gold, rose, bronze, white	sun	October–December in Central Texas; February–April in North Central Texas	spring–summer	Likes sandy soil. Does not transplant well. Spectacular blossoms. Often successful at self-sowing. Space at 6-inch intervals.
Portulaca (*P. grandiflora*)	6–12	shades of yellow, orange, rose, pink, white	sun	after frost-free date	summer–fall	It is difficult to think of a better annual for Central Texas. Preferring poor soil and heat, it produces rose-like blossoms in any sunny location. Very successful at self-sowing. Space at 6- to 8-inch intervals.
Rudbeckia, also called Brown-eyed Susan (*R. hybrida*)	24	yellow with brown center	sun	after frost-free date	summer–fall	Excellent cut flower. Transplants easily. Self-sowing. Space 12 to 15 inches apart.
Salpiglossis (*S. sinuata*)	24–36	gold, crimson, rose, blue	sun	after frost-free date	summer	Will not tolerate cold or heavy soil. Good cut flower; often known as Painted Tongue. Space 12 inches apart.

Name	Height (inches)	Color	Exposure	Planting Time	Blooming Time	Comments
Scarlet Sage (*Salvia splendens*)	18–36	scarlet	shade	after frost-free date	summer–fall	Excellent Central Texas choice. Vivid color can be overpowering if planted with other varieties. Plant at 12-inch intervals.
Snapdragon (*Antirrhinum* spp.)	18–24	assorted bright colors	sun to partial shade	October–December in Central Texas; February–April in North Central Texas	spring–summer	Likes well-fertilized soil. Try to buy rust-resistant varieties. Showy blossoms. Plant at 6- to 12-inch intervals.
Stock (*Matthiola incana*)	12–30	pink to purple	sun	October–December in Central Texas; February–April in North Central Texas	spring	Very fragrant. Excellent cut flower. Plant 8 inches apart.
Sweet Pea (*Lathyrus odoratus*)	48	many colors, also stripes	sun	October–December in Central Texas; February–April in North Central Texas	spring	Likes rich soil. Climbing varieties need support. Heat-resistant varieties: Cuthbertson, Galaxy, and Burpee's Giant Heat Resistant. Prefers cool weather. Plant 8 to 12 inches apart.

Name	Height (inches)	Color	Light	Planting date	Bloom time	Notes
Tithonia, also called **Mexican Sunflower** (*T. rotundifolia*)	48	orange, gold	sun	after frost-free date	summer	Heat- and drought-resistant. Although fast-growing, tithonia takes 3–4 months to produce a single flower. Plant 24 inches apart.
Wishbone (*Torenia fournieri*)	12	blue to deep purple	sun to partial shade	October–December in Central Texas; February–April in North Central Texas	spring–summer	Keep soil moist. Stamens bent in the shape of a chicken's wishbone, hence the name. Attractive two-lipped tubular blossom. Plant 6 to 8 inches apart.
Zinnia (*Z. spp.*)	12–36	apricot, yellow, rose, cream, red, orange	sun	after frost-free date	summer	Heat-tolerant. Excellent cut flower. Susceptible to mildew. Plant 6 to 12 inches apart.

Perennials

A long blooming season, low maintenance, and seemingly in-
finite variety leave little reason to wonder why perennials have
been a garden staple and favorite over the years.

PERENNIALS: CHRYSANTHEMUM, SHASTA DAISY, DAY LILY

Because perennials (broadly defined as herbaceous plants that
live three or more years) are around for a while, careful planning
is more important than it is with annuals, where a mistake just
needn't be repeated next year. This is particularly true for soil
preparation. While fertilizer can be applied periodically to restore
nutrients, soil texture is difficult to change once the flower bed has
been established. Clay soils in particular tend to get compacted
over the years, denying root systems air circulation. Very sandy
soils drain too rapidly for moisture-loving perennials. Soil preparation should include a two- to four-inch layer of compost, peat

moss, or decayed cow manure. The bed should be dug deeply (twelve to fifteen inches, ideally), and a light dressing of low-nitrogen fertilizer (abundant nitrogen at this time would burn the tender, young plants) and sulphur, copperas, iron sulfate, or lime in the case of highly acid soil, should be added and worked well into the soil. Other essential considerations when planning for perennials are height, color, blooming season, and exposure.

Although some perennials can be started from seed, many varieties that have been developed to produce very colorful blossoms only propagate asexually. Therefore, it makes sense to purchase container-grown or dormant bare-root plants at nurseries. Since most are easily propagated by division or cuttings (see propagation, chapter 3), the gardener has an excellent opportunity to increase his or her supply.

While container-raised plants can be planted almost any time but midsummer, if you buy bare-root perennials, they should be planted in the fall. When you plant, it is important that the hole be large enough to allow the roots to spread down and out. Container-grown plants should be planted at the same depth as they were in their pots. It is easy to determine how deeply to plant dormant plants by finding the soil mark from the previous season's growth. It is a good idea to insert support stakes for the taller perennials at planting time.

After planting, water thoroughly and make certain there are no air pockets. Mulch to conserve moisture, hold down weeds, and keep the soil temperature cool.

Care for perennials in successive years includes cultivation to aerate the soil and an application of 5–10–5 fertilizer in early spring and then again about six weeks later. Use a spading fork when cultivating, as it is less likely to damage roots and rhizomes than a hoe or spade.

Large blossoms can be encouraged by "disbudding" or removing all but the terminal buds. The blooming season for many perennials can be prolonged by removing spent blossoms.

Perennials

Name	Height (inches)	Color	Exposure	Blooming Season	Comments
Aster, also called Michaelmas Daisy (*A. novi-belgii*)	18–48	shades from blue to lavender to purple	sun	fall	This attractive, hardy plant will thrive in any well-drained soil. Spreading rapidly, it provides a profusion of blossoms. A good cut flower.
Carnation (*Dianthus caryophyllus*)	15–24	white, cream, orange, red, pink, lavender	sun	summer–fall	Because our summers are so hot, the carnation is often treated as a biennial here. It prefers light, sandy soil and should be fertilized every other month.
Chrysanthemum (*C. spp.*)	12–36	white, cream, rust, yellow, maroon	sun	late summer–fall	Easily started from cuttings in spring, this fall bloomer needs soil well worked with organic matter. Makes good cut flower or potted plant. Nice scent.
Coneflower (*Rudbeckia spp.*)	24–36	yellow	sun to partial	summer–fall	Excellently adapted to Central Texas conditions, the coneflower's height

Name	Height	Color	Light	Season	Remarks
			shade		makes it an ideal background flower. Good cut flower.
Coreopsis (*C.* spp.)	12–36	yellow	sun	summer	One must be careful not to overfertilize the soil coreopsis grows in. Clumps should be divided in spring after two to three years of flowering. Needs little care.
Daisy, Gerber (*Gerbera jamesonii*)	12–18	many	sun to partial shade	spring–fall	These long-lasting, long-stemmed blossoms make excellent cut flowers. Apply 5–10–5 fertilizer bimonthly. Be careful not to cover crowns when planting, or plant will fail to bloom.
Daisy, Shasta (*Chrysanthemum maximum*)	12–36	white	sun to partial shade	summer–fall	Excellent as a cut flower, the double form has a gay, feathery appearance. Divide every three to four years to keep vital.
Day Lily (*Hemerocallis* spp.)	15–36	yellow to orange and pink to mahogany	sun to partial shade	spring–summer	Not a true lily, but rather a fleshy-rooted herb, the day lily is noted for its ease of culture. Ideally planted in humus-enriched loam and fertilized

Name	Height (inches)	Color	Exposure	Blooming Season	Comments
					with a 12–12–12 mix in spring or early summer, it can thrive under conditions of neglect. Divide in spring or fall after every four to six years.
Delphinium (*D. spp.*)	12–72	white, pink, blue	sun	spring	The medium-sized strains are preferred because they require less support and make a better sized cut flower. Delphinium is often treated as an annual in this region. The seed is sown in early fall, and plants will bloom the following spring.
Hollyhock (*Althaea rosea*)	48–72	red, rose, yellow, white	full sun	summer	A favorite of days-gone-by, the hollyhock looks best when planted in rows against a fence or similar background. Set 12 to 24 inches apart. Indian Spring variety is annual.
Moss Phlox (*P. subulata*)	4–5	white, pink, lavender	sun	early spring	An excellent rock garden plant, this specimen of phlox (sometimes called "thrift" in nurseries) prefers humus-enriched, moist soil. Clumps can be

divided after spring flowers fade. Foliage then should be clipped halfway back to aid root recovery.

Name	Height	Color	Light	Blooming Season	Remarks
Peony (*Paeonia officinalis*)	24–42	white, pink, shades of red	one-half day sun	spring	A long-time favorite perennial in cool-climate gardens, the peony can be grown in the northern part of our region, around Dallas and Fort Worth. Its striking blossoms make beautiful cut flowers and are also fragrant. Plant so that the crown is only an inch below the surface. Plant in fall. Feed monthly, February through August, with 5–10–5 fertilizer and give bone meal in November and May.
Peruvian Verbena (*V. peruviana*)	12–20	pink to red	full sun	late spring through fall	An extraordinarily long blooming season and a trailing growth habit make this lovely plant an ideal flowering ground cover for sunny areas. Good tolerance to heat and drought.
Plantain Lily (*Hosta* spp.)	18–24	white	sun to deep shade, with partial	summer–fall	While a small, attractive lilylike flower is produced, most people plant *hosta* for its broad-leaf foliage and because it does so well in places where few other plants survive.

Name	Height (inches)	Color	Exposure	Blooming Season	Comments
Plumbago (*Plumbago capensis*)	18–30	centian blue	sun to partial shade	summer–fall	Having a bushy growth habit, this is a profuse bloomer that does extremely well in our heat and sun. It will die back in winter, but new growth will appear from the roots in spring. Fast spreading, it is easily divided.
Salvia (*S.* spp.)	24–48	shades from blue to violet	sun	summer–fall	All salvias produce excellent cut flowers and are easily propagated from seeds, stem cuttings, or by division. The popular annual is scarlet sage (see annuals list, this chapter).
Statice (*Limonium latifolium*)	18–24	lavender	sun	summer	Stalks of delicate flowers give statice a feathery appearance. Serves well as a border plant or cut flower.
Violet (*Viola* spp.)	3–8	lavender to violet	partial shade	spring and fall	Masses of broad, heart-shaped evergreen leaves and a low growth habit make the violet a favorite ground cover. Prefers rich, moist soil.

shade preferred

Bulbs

Although many bulb plants are perennials, they are often treated separately in gardening literature because of the special way in which they store nutrients for the next growing season.

BULBS: RANUNCULUS, ANEMONE, HYACINTH, CROCUS

Bulbs are not roots but rather, modified, underground stems. Other forms of underground stems that function similarly are corms, rhizomes, and tubers. Tuberous roots, while true roots, will also be discussed in this section.

Good drainage for bulbs is essential, not just preferred. If you cannot meet this requirement, don't risk it; try something else. When preparing beds for bulbs, cultivate to a minimum depth of six to twelve inches. Dig in a good amount of organic material in the form of compost, well-rotted manure, or peat to make a good bottom layer, as the bulbs will send out roots twice the depth at which they were planted. At this time, work in a high-phosphate fertilizer such as superphosphate or bone meal to ensure good root development. A good rule of thumb for planting is that bulbs are planted at a depth roughly 2½ times their diameter. In heavy soils, they can be planted slightly less deep. Generally bulbs should be planted broader base at the bottom and tip pointing up. Exceptions are noted on the chart that follows. Most bulbs are planted from mid-October through December. The caladium, an exception, is planted in spring. Water thoroughly after planting, and mulch. If the winter is a dry one, don't forget to water the beds.

After the flowers have faded, the bulbs will benefit from an application of 5–10–5 fertilizer. Do not remove the foliage, which is producing nourishment for the next season's growth, until it has yellowed and dried. Some bulbs should be replaced every year, while others may be left in the ground. Then there are those which should be dug up, properly stored, and replanted the next fall (see chart that follows). Before you store them, you should allow bulbs to dry for a week in a dark, well-ventilated area. Residual soil should be removed, and the bulbs then stored in a paper bag or unsealed box filled with dry peat moss or vermiculite. Bulbs should be stored in a cool, dark location.

Bulbs and Their Relatives

Name	Root Form	Height (inches)	Color	Planting Depth (inches)	Exposure	Blooming Season	Comments
Amaryllis, also called Belladonna Lily (*A. belladonna*)	bulb	36	red	3–4	sun	April–May	Thriving in the poor soils of the west, the amaryllis produces splendid blossoms and is bothered by very few pests. Bulb can remain in the ground year after year.
Anemone, also called Poppy Anemone (*A. coronaria*)	tuber	10–18	red, white, purple, stripes	2	sun to partial shade	early spring	Bright, poppylike blossoms distinguish this early spring bloomer. The anemone is most successful when treated as an annual and started with new tubers each year. Excellent cut flower. The sharp, distinctive point should be positioned downward when planted.
Begonia, Tuberous (*B. tuberhybrida*)	tuber	6–10	pink, red, white	2	filtered sunlight	summer	Tubers should be started indoors in January. After frost-free date in March, plants may be transplanted to a location that gets filtered sunlight. The planting medium should consist of one-half organic matter and one-

Name	Root Form	Height (inches)	Color	Planting Depth (inches)	Exposure	Blooming Season	Comments
							half coarse sand. Soil must be kept moist for begonias to succeed in our climate. Additional plants may be taken from stem cuttings. Tubers should be dug up in November and stored. Plant with root hairs growing downward.
Caladium (*C.* spp.)	tuber	12–15	multi-colored foliage	2–3	shade	summer–fall	Plant caladiums in the spring when the days and nights are warm. As the tubers tend to rot, dig up after foliage has died back and store properly. Colorful and good performance in shady places has made caladium a popular landscape addition.
Canna (*C. generalis*)	tuberous root	48–60	white, yellow, coral, red	3	sun	summer–fall	Plant in spring when danger of frost has passed. Cannas look best planted in groups. To keep best appearance, pick faded blossoms. Divide in spring.

Name	Type			Color	Light	Planting time	Notes
Crocus (*C.* spp.)	corm	6	2–3	white, yellow, blue, pink	sun to partial shade	fall or spring	Provides sprightly blossoms when little else is in bloom. Most successful in the northern area of our region. Insufficient cold will result in failure to bloom. Corms may remain in ground year-round.
Daffodil (*Narcissus* spp.)	bulb	15	4–5	yellow and cream	sun	early spring	Daffodils and other members of the *Narcissus* genus like colder winters than some parts of Central Texas normally get. In these areas it may be necessary to plant new bulbs each year.
Day Lily (see perennials, this chapter)							
Dahlia (*D.* spp.)	tuberous root	24–96	5–6	most colors except blue	sun	summer	Wait for soil to warm before planting tubers. Stake to support taller varieties. Spectacular blossoms two to eight inches across will bloom all summer. Dig up and store tubers after foliage has yellowed and died. Two to four weeks before planting in

Name	Root Form	Height (inches)	Color	Planting Depth (inches)	Exposure	Blooming Season	Comments
							spring, divide the tuber and dust with sulphur to prevent rot. Plant tuber on its side with the eye pointed upward.
Four-O'clock (*Mirabilis jalapa*)	tuberous root	24-36	white, yellow, red	2-4	sun	summer–fall	Can be treated as an annual and started from seed. If you choose to cultviate as a perennial, follow culture comments for dahlia. Fragrant flower, open in late afternoon.
Gladiolus (*G.* spp.)	corm	48-72	red, white, pink, yellow	6	sun	summer	The spikes of showy flowers make excellent cut flowers. Store corms in cool, dark place during the winter. Stake for support. Thrips, a common problem, can be controlled with malathion.
Hyacinth (*Hyacinthus* spp.)	bulb	6-15	blue, purple, lavender,	4-5	sun to partial shade	spring	Plant late October to early December. If bulbs are allowed to remain in the ground, the blossoms will be progressively smaller each year. There-

Name	Type	Height (in.)	Color	Depth (in.)	Light	Bloom	Comments
			white			spring	fore it is best to buy new bulbs each year.
Iris, Bearded (*I.* spp.)	rhizome	15–36	broad spectrum of colors from light to dark	tops of rhizomes planted just below the surface	sun to partial shade	spring	Plant bearded iris in late August or September. Apply a low-nitrogen, high-phosphorous fertilizer such as 0-20-20 in spring, as growth begins, and then again after blooming. Do not allow plants to dry out. Bearded irises should be divided every three to four years to prevent overcrowded conditions which affect the size and quality of the flowers.
Iris, Dutch (*I.* spp.)	bulb	12–24	blue, white, yellow	4	sun	spring	Plant bulbs October through November. Like bearded iris, they should be fertilized with a high-phosphorous fertilizer before and after blooming. Dig up bulbs and replant every three to four years.
Jonquil (*Narcissus* spp.)	bulb	15	many shades of yellow	4–5	sun	early spring	Smaller than the true daffodil but more common in the South, jonquils look best when planted in drifts or masses.

Name	Root Form	Height (inches)	Color	Planting Depth (inches)	Exposure	Blooming Season	Comments
Lily (*Lilium* spp.)	bulb	15–36	white, yellow, orange, mahogany	6	sun to partial shade	summer	Most lilies do best in porous, rich, moist soil that is slightly acid. Because they are never totally dormant, the fragile bulbs should be handled gently and planted as soon after purchase as possible. Mulching to conserve moisture is important. Some varieties that are good for this area are Madonna (tolerates moderate alkalinity), Regal, Martagon hybrids, and Tiger.
Oxalis (*O.* spp.)	bulb	8	pink to rose-red, yellow	2	partial shade	spring–summer	Rapidly spreading its appealing cloverlike foliage, this cultivated cousin of one of our prevalent wild flowers is valued for its long blooming season and shade tolerance. Plant in August or September when dormant. Oxalis bulbs remain in soil throughout the year.

Name	Type	Height	Color	Light	Season	Notes
Ranunculus (*R. asiaticus*)	tuber	15–24	yellow, orange, red, pink, white	sun	early spring	Plant with tuber prongs in a downward position in moist, humus-enriched soil. After foliage has died, tubers may be dug up and stored until replanted in October to December; or you may treat ranunculus as an annual, starting with new tubers each fall. The beautiful camellialike blossom makes an excellent cut flower.
Tulip (*Tulipa* spp.)	bulb	6–30	white, shades of red, yellow, purple	sun	spring	Preferring other climates and physical conditions, the tulip will produce fine, classic blossoms if given special attention. Bulbs should be stored in the bottom of the refrigerator for four to six weeks prior to planting in December. Soil should be light and enriched with a high-phosphorous fertilizer. Buy new bulbs each year.

Wild Flowers—A Gardening Alternative

One does not have to be a particularly sensitive soul to be aware that Texas is a veritable flower basket. More than four thousand species of flowering plants have been identified in her varied regions, "where they smile in secret, looking over wasted lands."[1] Wild flower societies, the Texas State Highway Department, and commercial wild flower seed purveyors do their best to help the people of Texas enjoy this renewable resource.

Most species of wild flowers look their best when planted in masses, and a bed of wild flowers offers the gardener or homeowner an attractive landscape option. However, being aware of their demands, strengths, and weaknesses before you broadcast the front yard with bluebonnets will spare you disappointment. While they give the impression of being just about indestructible when growing in a crack in the sidewalk, don't be fooled into thinking that these flowers would do much better in your well-fertilized, regularly watered flower bed. For many wild flowers, the crack in the sidewalk is the perfect environment—and a difficult one for the gardener to duplicate. Another formidable reason you do not see more wild flower gardens in suburban settings is that, while so beautiful and striking when in bloom, many a wild flower looks like an unwanted weed a good part of the year. Conscientious wild flower fanciers can compensate by planting a succession of seasonal flowers.

Seed for wild flowers can be either purchased from a seedsman specializing in wild flowers and native plants or collected in the fields. If you do the latter, identify and mark the flower when it is in bloom, and return later in the season when the seed is ready for harvest, usually about six weeks after flowering.

DIRECTIONS FOR PLANTING WILD FLOWERS

1. Plant at the correct time (when the flowers are sowing their seeds) and in soil and lighting conditions similar to those in which the flower is ordinarily found.

[1]Alfred, Lord Tennyson, "Song of the Lotos-Eaters."

2. Cultivate the soil surface to allow the seedlings to get a foothold.
3. Cover seedlings lightly with soil, and firm gently.
4. Water lightly.

A light dusting with a general fungicide and/or insecticide will improve your chances of a successful bouquet. Hard-shelled seeds —for example, bluebonnets—will benefit from a twenty-four-hour soaking in warm water before you plant them. Remember that the germination rate for wild flowers is below that of the packet of marigolds you buy at the nursery.

Below are listed a few of the more spectacular and easier to grow wild flowers.

Bluebonnets (*Lupinus* spp.). The official state flower needs no introduction. Heralding spring, its spikes of blue with white blossoms almost seem to cover the earth during years of adequate rainfall. The bluebonnet most prevalent in our area (*L. subcarnosus*) can grow to fifteen inches and is an ideal companion to the Indian paintbrush. Seeds may planted July through September.

Coreopsis (*C.* spp.). The cheerful yellow rays and dark brown centers of the daisylike coreopsis brighten the byways from spring through summer. Most species grow from eight to twenty-four inches tall. Planted in spring or fall, coreopsis makes a good companion for firewheels and Mexican hats.

Firewheel, also called **Indian Blanket** (*Gaillardia pulchella*). The brilliant yellow to orange to pink hues of the firewheel's rays easily identify this prolific member of the daisy family. Growing from eight to sixteen inches, its regular season is May to June, although it can be found often at other times of the year. That is a wild flower's prerogative. Seed can be sown from fall to early spring.

Gayfeather (*Liatris* spp.). Spikes of rose-purple flowers decorate the early fall landscape. Attaining a height of three to four feet, this conspicuous North American native grows best in dry, sandy soils. Seed should be sown in fall.

Indian Paintbrush (*Castilleja indivisa*). So often seen and associated with the bluebonnet, this splendid early spring bloomer

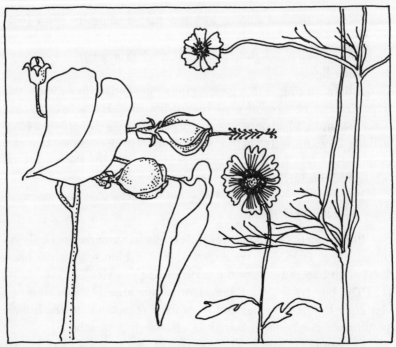

WILD FLOWERS: TURK'S CaP, FIREWHEEL, COREOPSIS

is a root parasite that requires its own planting procedure. Seeds should be sown during the fall in holes punched in grassy fields or lawns, covered lightly, and watered. Although difficult to start, an established stand of the red-orange spiked blossoms will please for years.

Mexican Hat (*Ratibida columnaris*). Yellow rays hang down from a dark brown disk, giving the Mexican hat the appearance of a black-eyed Susan who went wrong. Showing up in just about any sunny location, this flower blooms all summer long. Not fussy about soil, Mexican hat can be sown from fall to spring.

Turk's Cap (*Malvaviscus drummondii*). Besides having a delightful little blossom, the Turk's cap has one other advantage over many other wild flowers: lush, abundant foliage. Blooming from April through October, the flower has bright red petals that do not unfold but remain loosely coiled around the projecting stamens and style. Capable of attaining a height of ten feet, it looks best when pruned back after two years. Seeds should be sown in the fall, or the plant may be started from softwood cuttings in early summer. It is shade-tolerant but freezes back in the winter.

Winecups (*Callirhoë* spp.). With a pleasing cuplike shape and an intense burgundy hue, the winecup is an undeniably beautiful flower. Its low-growing, attractive foliage makes it a desirable cultivated plant, particularly well suited for hanging baskets. Seeds are sown in fall.

A Vegetable Primer

Earth in her heart laughs, looking at the heaven,
Thinking of the harvest, I look and think of mine.
G. Meredith, "Love in the Valley"

VEGETABLE gardening is so much more than planting seeds and harvesting vegetables for the table. To us, it is a microcosm of life, representing its joys, frustrations, failures, and successes. The appeal of nurturing something to the finished product is so basic that even gardeners who fail (in terms of their own expectations) seldom can resist the temptation to try again next season.

Certainly, we do not mean to emphasize the intangible, therapeutic benefits of vegetable gardening over the tangible results. In many instances store-bought vegetables simply cannot match the freshness of homegrown varieties. How often have you been disappointed by the flavor of that perfectly spherical, brilliant red tomato or by the toughness of the green beans purchased at the supermarket? Today, with growing fields so far removed from the market, many commercial varieties are selected for their eye appeal and ability to withstand shipment in good condition rather than for flavor or texture.

PLANNING

Good planning is the bottom line to successful vegetable gardening. A good look at the demands—cultivating, watering, fertilizing, pest-control regimen—of a garden will help the gardener decide how much time he wants to devote to the venture.

After this commitment has been made, it is time to make a site selection based on the physical limitations of your yard. (Some communities rent garden space on public land. This is a boon to apartment dwellers and those who are unable to garden at home for other reasons. Check to see if your local government provides this service.) The requirements of a vegetable garden are good soil, sufficient sunlight (at least six hours), adequate water, proper spacing, and appropriate temperature. In addition, your vegetable plot should be located as far from trees as possible. Not only do they shade the area, but their far-ranging root systems compete for nutrients.

Temperature is usually the only condition over which the gardener has no control. So, while other factors affect where you place your garden, temperature will be a major determinant in choosing vegetable varieties that are suitable for our area of Texas and in deciding the dates for planting. Finally, if you prefer organic gardening, you may want to acquaint yourself with those plants which suffer relatively little damage from pests and with the methods that effectively deal with some of the more common problemmakers. Carrots, parsnips, leeks, endive, asparagus, and radishes survive quite well without any assistance from insecticides. In spite of all your careful planning, though, the realistic expectation of some plant loss is the best bulwark against disappointment. The home gardener is lucky in that he can afford to make some difficult choices that the farmer cannot. What do you do about the large, green-black-and-gold-striped caterpillar that happily devours your parsley? This creature, left alone, will develop into the beautiful black swallowtail butterfly.

When planning your garden, remember that vegetable crops are categorized by their preferred growing season. The cool-season plants, generally the leafy and root vegetables, prefer to put on their vegetative growth at temperatures ten to fifteen degrees below those preferred by the warm-season crops. We harvest radishes, carrots, lettuce, asparagus, cabbage, and broccoli before they are fully developed plants. Increasing temperatures and longer days will prompt these plants to "bolt," or go into flower and fruit production. Normally, cool-season plants can be planted the latter part of February.

The warm-season vegetables, those whose fruit we eat, need warmer temperatures at day and night for germination and the ripening of fruit. If set out before the days are warm enough, these plants will grow very slowly until the conditions are right. Examples of warm-season crops are beans, eggplant, tomatoes, corn, melons, and squash. If your garden has partial shade sometime during the day, it is a good idea to plant the leafy or root vegetables in that area, leaving the fruit and flower crops to soak in all the sun. In our climate, warm-season crops are more reliable, but careful attention to the varieties appropriate for our area will assure success for many of the cool-season vegetables as well.

GARDEN PREPARATION

Vegetable gardens require more attention in preparation than flower beds or areas where shrubs are to be grown. A soil sample to analyze your soil's pH and nutrient needs is a proper beginning. Soil-testing kits for do-it-yourselfers are available at most local nurseries, but better still, as we have mentioned, is the soil-testing service available through your county agent (see chapter 2). The convenient mail-in kit provides everything you need and comes with excellent instructions. Recommendations will be made in accordance with the desired use of the soil, i.e., vegetable garden, lawn, shrubs, flowers. Your results will be returned within a few weeks. We recommend getting this chore done some time in the winter.

Following the recommendations of the soil analysis, you need to add the necessary fertilizer and to work the soil to an appropriate texture. The soil must be friable to allow the root systems to get good anchorage and to branch properly. If the soil is too hard or compacted, poor root development will result in stunted or deformed root vegetables, a common problem with carrots. This problem can sometimes be avoided by growing root crops in raised beds. When you plant them directly in the ground, you should dig the soil deeply or rototill it if you are cultivating a large plot. Soil conditioners such as sand, peat, compost, and rotted manure should be added and worked in well. When adding the fertilizer, be sure to follow the label instructions for the amount. Now water thoroughly, as the soil should be moist (preferably to a depth of two to three feet) at the time of planting, not afterward. Let the garden settle for about a week to avoid fertilizer burn.

Do not work in wet soil—even if it means delaying your planting a bit. Not only is wet soil difficult and unpleasant to work in, but it is also counterproductive. Heavy, wet soil is easily compacted.

The sketch on page 172 shows one plan for a vegetable garden. Note the placement of the channels allowing the gardener to use the space between smaller crops, such as herbs, lettuce, and radishes. This size garden is large enough to provide vegetables for a family of three or four and will not overwork the gardener with demanding chores—a sure way to sap enthusiasm.

What about gardens, though, for people who live in apartments, condominiums, townhouses, or executive homes? Residents of these increasingly popular housing styles need not deny themselves the pleasures or fruitful results of vegetable gardening. Appropriate containers, adequate sunlight, and high-yield crops are the patio or balcony gardener's foremost considerations. Clay pots or redwood boxes are excellent choices. If you construct your own containers from wood, be sure to provide for adequate drainage, avoid highly toxic wood preservatives, and use galvanized hardware.

Because apartment dwellers seldom have more than one or two points of exposure, the amount of available sunlight will be the most limiting factor in plant selection. If your only exposure is a northern one and you are determined to garden, be realistic and try parsley, chives, or mint instead of tomatoes or cucumbers, which will never make it.

Some suitable vegetable varieties for containers are: peppers (both bell and jalapeno), tomatoes (particularly the smaller cherry and patio varieties), chard, lettuce, radishes, and the shorter varieties of carrots. Cucumbers require eighteen inches of soil and need to be trained to a trellis, but they will produce extravagantly. All container-grown vegetables need to be watered and fertilized more frequently than garden-grown vegetables. However, weeding and harvesting chores are far easier.

To keep soil in the garden from becoming packed down, we recommend using the channeling method described by W. G. Smith

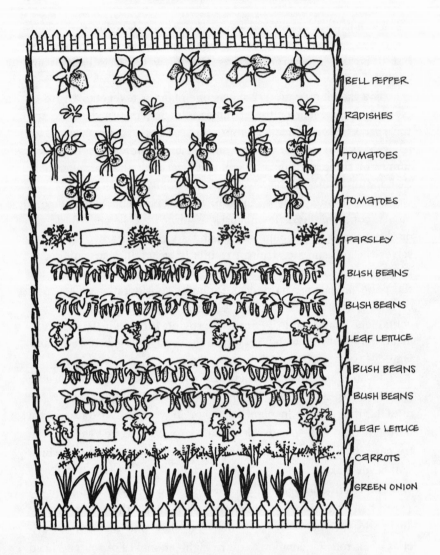

BELL PEPPER

RADISHES

TOMATOES

TOMATOES

PARSLEY

BUSH BEANS

BUSH BEANS

LEAF LETTUCE

BUSH BEANS

BUSH BEANS

LEAF LETTUCE

CARROTS

GREEN ONION

SAMPLE VEGETABLE GARDEN

WITH CHANNELS

in *Gardening for Food*.[1] Briefly, this procedure advises placing standard concrete blocks (sixteen inches by eight inches by two inches) in a row sixteen inches apart, with roughly twenty-eight inches between rows. This will form a channel that will permit you to reach any plant in the garden without compacting the soil between rows. It also allows additional planting in the spaces between the blocks.

PLANTING

Now that your plans and soil preparations are complete, it is time to plant. This has always been our favorite part of gardening. Ah, the air of expectation! Years ago, toward the end of winter, gardeners set out cold frames and started seeds indoors in flats. These methods are just as good today as they were then and are still the most economical for large gardens. But gardening has changed, and so has the typical gardener. Standard lots are smaller now, and gardeners have less time. Nurseries carry young plants of endless varieties at low prices. It doesn't seem to make sense to set out a flat, buy a package of seed, and take careful, tender care of seedlings if you need only three or four pepper plants.

When you buy young vegetable plants from a nursery, it is very important to make sure they are strong and vigorous. Here bargains are not always bargains. Some plants clearly look shopworn: they are wilted, the bottom leaves are yellowing, and roots extend far beyond the limits of the container. Spring is a busy time at nurseries, and often some chores just get neglected. A very common problem with such plants is that they have been allowed to dry out. The containers are small, and unless they are watered regularly they dry out rapidly. Beware of plants with soil that looks hard and has withdrawn from the container walls. Stock is important, and when you start from seed, this is under your control.

TENDING

After sowing the seed in flats or outside, following the directions on the seed packet, you can just sit back and wait, making

[1]W. G. Smith, *Gardening for Food* (New York: Charles Scribner's Sons, 1972), pp. 64–66.

sure your garden does not dry out. When the plants are well on their way, it is time to mulch. In our hot, dry, and windy climate, this practice cannot be overemphasized. Mulching with clean straw, bark mulch, dried grass clippings, or sawdust will conserve moisture and, if you turn them under at the end of the season, add organic material to the soil. Black plastic is a useful mulch for strawberries, squash, and other fruits and vegetables that tend to rot when they sit on wet soil. Mulching is also an effective weed control.

Throughout the growing seasons (remember we have two of them), your vegetables will need new applications of fertilizer. Side dressings of small amounts at more frequent intervals are better than larger applications less frequently. This is particularly true in sandy soils, where moisture retention is poor. Follow the directions on your fertilizer label. From time to time, you will need to cope with insect invaders and/or diseases (see chapter 13). Again, the first line of defense is a well-kept garden, one free of debris. Collars made from tin cans surrounding young plants, sprays concocted from foul-smelling ingredients such as garlic, hot peppers, onions, and marigolds; importing natural predators; and companion planting with naturally repellent flowers and herbs work to varying degrees. When you resort to applying pesticides, never exceed label instructions, which will tell you the number of days before harvest you may apply the chemical. It is a good idea to refrain from using chlorinated hydrocarbons in the vegetable garden when other products are available; they break down very slowly, and sometimes into other toxic chemicals. Therefore, they should be reserved for other uses.

TIPS

No matter how many garden books you read, something for which you are totally unprepared will always come up. Often these experiences seem so simple it is easy to get angry at yourself for missing the obvious or at others for not warning you. It's the accumulation of such experience that really makes a gardener. We would like to pass on a few such tips—though not enough to take the fun out of learning for yourself.

Asparagus: Once established, this delicately flavored and expensive vegetable just keeps going. Planting of roots is arduous, and deep soil is required, but the harvest is well worth it for fans. Shop carefully for roots; a survey of local nurseries revealed a great difference in quality. Harvest for eight to ten weeks in spring, then allow plants to rest before harvesting again in fall.

Beans: Beans do well here, and it's difficult not to succeed with them. Rust, a fungus, can be a problem, though, and you should take care to prevent it from spreading by avoiding touching wet plants.

Broccoli: If you are starting this plant from seed, it can take up to five months to mature, so get a good start. Remember to harvest while the heads are still hard and green. If you have never seen a broccoli plant in flower, it might be fun to let one go to seed.

Carrots: The seed is delicate, and the germination rate is not always good, so be sure to buy seed dated for the proper season. Seed tape is a good buy for carrots. In our heavy clay soils, deformed carrots are common. Purchase a recommended variety and try to avoid walking between rows as much as possible to keep from compacting the soil. Carrots do not like dry weather.

Corn: Don't plan on planting a few stalks of corn. Corn depends on wind for pollination, and without enough plants to fill the air with pollen it will be a hit-or-miss affair. For this reason, corn in a home garden should be planted in hills or small groups rather than in one or two long rows. Corn earworms are almost as much a part of corn as the tassle. Sevin sprayed on the silks soon after they appear and then again in about a week is a good control. People who know vegetables tell you to have the water boiling before you pick the corn. They are quite right. The sugar in corn begins to turn into starch immediately after the corn has been picked; for that reason, store-bought corn never can be as sweet as homegrown.

Cucumbers: This is a good plant to grow in a tub or other container. That way, it is easy to provide the rich, loamy soil and water it prefers. It's also a good way to keep this aggressive vine from invading space that belongs to other plants in the garden.

Lettuce: So easy and quick to grow is this salad favorite that one can sow seed in flower beds. Pill bugs love the new leaves, so watch out. Recommended varieties are essential to avoid untimely bolting.

Melons: Melons require lots of time, sun, and space. It is best to water in deep furrows to avoid soaking the fruit. Sometimes pollination is difficult and a helping hand is necessary from the gardener.

Onions: Seed should be planted in Central Texas between mid-September and mid-October. Young plants available at nurseries in late winter and early spring are fine but will yield a smaller bulb. Check the chart at the end of this chapter for proper planting times for seeds and sets.

Peas, Garden. In our small suburban plot, we finally gave the space to crops with higher yields after harvesting enough peas for two meals annually. It takes a lot of peas to make a meal. Fortunately, the recently developed sugar snap pea promises to eliminate this serious drawback to planting peas in small gardens. Sweet and plump, sugar snap peas are excellent raw in salads, steamed or boiled, or stir-fried for oriental dishes. The four- to six-foot vines do require trellising.

Peppers: Whether a hot jalapeno or a sweet bell, peppers like our heat and do very well here. Mosaic, whose symptoms are yellowing and hard, shrivelled leaves, is a common problem. The best control is to remove the affected plant.

Potatoes: Consider this space robber only if you have a large garden.

Radish: Tough and quick, the radish comes as close to being a can't-fail vegetable as anything we can think of.

Spinach: This a tough one in our region, where summer can come upon us so suddenly. Spinach is definitely a cool-season crop, and many gardeners prefer growing chard here. Be sure to use only the recommended varieties.

Squash: Who has not received surplus zucchini from gardening friends and neighbors? Given a half-day of sun and adequate water, applied with a soaker hose to avoid soaking the crowns, this cucurbit family member is a most willing provider. To keep young fruit from rotting, provide some means (e.g., plastic cover on the ground, upturned flower pots) of preventing contact with the soil. The squash is bothered by several pests—cucumber beetle, pickleworm, and the deadly squash vine borer. Some success may be expected from applications of Sevin and diazinon.

Tomatoes: Surely here is the queen of the vegetable garden. So many nice, new varieties are available that there is a tomato for every type of gardener. Check your nursery for wilt- and nematode-resistant varieties. Tomatoes require lots of sun and good drainage. Overwatering may result in blossom drop. Avoid setting out plants too early. Fruit will not set when night temperature drops below fifty-five degrees. Conversely, neither will it set when daytime temperatures approach one hundred degrees. Tomato plants do not like nicotine, so avoid smoking while tending them.

Vegetable Varieties for Central Texas

Beans, lima: Florida Butter (pole), Fordhook 242 (bush), Henderson Bush, Jackson Wonder (bush), Sieva (Carolina) (pole)

Beans, pinto: Luna, Pinto III

Beans, snap: Blue Lake (bush), Contender (bush), Dade (pole), Extender (bush), Kentucky Wonder (pole), Stringless Blue Lake (pole), Tendercrop (bush), Topcrop (bush)

Beets: Asgrow Wonder, Detroit Dark Red, Green Top Bunching

Broccoli: DeCicco, Topper 43, Waterham 29

Brussels sprouts: Jade Cross

Cabbage: Drumhead (savoy), Early Jersey Wakefield (hybrid), Early Round Dutch, Glove, Golden Acre, Gourmet (hybrid), Market Prize (hybrid), Red Rock (red), Rio Verde (hybrid)

Cantaloupe: Golden Perfection, Hale's Best, Perlita, Rio Gold, Smith's Perfect

Carrot: Danvers 126, Imperator, Nantes, Red Core Chantenay

Cauliflower: Snowball

Chard: Fordhook, Lucullus

Collards: Georgia, Vates

Corn: Bonanza, Buttersweet, Calumet, Country Gentlemen (white), Golden Security, Merit, Silver Queen (white)

Cucumbers: Ashley (slicer), Bravo (pickling), Crispy (pickling), National Pickling, Palomar (slicer), Picadilly (pickling), Poinsett (slicer), Straight 8 (slicer)

Eggplant: Black Beauty, Black Knight, Florida Market

Garlic: Texas White

Kale: Dwarf Blue Curled, Vates

Lettuce, head: Great Lakes, Valverde

Lettuce, leaf: Salad Bowl, Oakleaf, Ruby (red)

Lettuce, butterhead: Summer Bibb, Tendercrisp

Lettuce, Romaine: Valmaine

Mustard: Florida Broadleaf, Southern Giant Curled, Tendergreen

Okra: Clemson Spineless, Emerald, Louisiana Green Velvet

Onion: Beltsville Bunching, Crystal Wax, Eclipse, Granes (yellow and white), Grano 502 (green)

Parsley: Evergreen, Moss Curled

Peas, English: Alaska, Little Marvel, Wando

Peas, southern: Blackeye No. 5, Burgundy (purple hull), Chamion (cream), Cream 40

Peas, sugar snap

Pepper, sweet: Bellringer, California Wonder, Emerald Giant, Keystone Giant, Yolo Wonder

Pepper, hot: Hungarian Wax, Jalapeño, Long Red or Thin Cayenne, Texas Serano

Potato, sweet: Centennial, Copperskin Goldrush, Jewel, Porto Rico

Potato, Irish: Kennebec (white), Red Lasoda (red)

Radish: Black Spanish, Cherry Belle, Early Scarlet Globe (short top), White Chinese, White Icicle (winter)

Spinach: Bloomsdale, Dixie Savoy, Early Hybrid 7

Squash: Acorn (winter), Butternut (winter), Dixie Hybrid Crookneck, Early Prolific Straightneck, White Buck

Tomato (standard-sized): Better Boy, Bonus, Homestead 24, Nematex (nematode-resistant), Porter, Rutgers, Saladette, Spring Giant, TAMU Monte Grande, Terrific, Walters

Turnip: Purple Top, Seven Top, White Globe

Watermelon: Charleston Gray, Jubilee, Sugar Baby, Sweet Princess

Suggested Planting Dates, Space Requirements, Light Requirements, and Maturity Rates for Vegetables

Crop	Planting Dates (in relation to the last [spring] and first [fall] freeze dates)*		Space Requirements	Light Requirements	Maturity Rate**
	Spring	Fall			
Asparagus (roots)	4 to 6 weeks before	——	large	partial shade	perennial
Beans, Lima	up to 4 weeks after	8 to 10 weeks before	small	sun	moderate
Beans, Snap	up to 4 weeks after	14 to 16 weeks before	small	sun	fast
Beets	4 to 6 weeks before	8 to 10 weeks before	small	partial shade	fast
Broccoli	4 to 6 weeks before	10 to 16 weeks before	small	sun	moderate
Brussels Sprouts	4 to 6 weeks before	10 to 14 weeks before	small	partial shade	slow
Cabbage	4 to 6 weeks before	10 to 16 weeks before	small	partial shade	slow
Cabbage, Chinese	4 to 6 weeks before	12 to 14 weeks before	small	partial shade	moderate
Carrot	4 to 6 weeks before	10 to 16 weeks before	small	partial shade	moderate
Cauliflower	——	10 to 16 weeks before	large	sun	slow
Celery and Celeriac	——	12 to 16 weeks before	small	sun	slow
Chard	2 to 6 weeks before	12 to 16 weeks before	small	partial shade	moderate
Collards	2 to 6 weeks before	8 to 12 weeks before	large	partial shade	slow
Corn, Sweet	up to 6 weeks after	12 to 14 weeks before	large	sun	moderate to slow
Cucumber	up to 6 weeks after	10 to 12 weeks before	large	sun	moderate
Dandelion	2 to 6 weeks before	4 to 10 weeks before	small	partial shade	slow

Endive, Curly	4 to 6 weeks before	8 to 12 weeks before	small	partial shade	slow
Fennel, Florence	———	10 to 16 weeks before	small	sun	moderate
Garlic	2 to 6 weeks before	4 to 6 weeks before	small	sun	slow
Kale	2 to 6 weeks before	8 to 10 weeks before	small	partial shade	fast
Kohlrabi	2 to 6 weeks before	12 to 16 weeks before	small	partial shade	moderate
Leeks	2 to 8 weeks before	———	small	sun	slow
Lettuce, Head	6 weeks before to 2 weeks after	10 to 14 weeks before	small	partial shade	slow
Lettuce, Leaf	6 weeks before to 2 weeks after	10 to 12 weeks before	small	partial shade	fast
Melon, Cantaloupe	up to 6 weeks after	14 to 16 weeks before	large	sun	slow
Mustard	up to 6 weeks after	10 to 16 weeks before	small	partial shade	fast
Okra	2 to 6 weeks after	12 to 16 weeks before	large	sun	moderate
Onion, Bermuda (bedding plants)	4 to 10 weeks before	———	small	sun	moderate
Onion, Bermuda (seed)	6 to 8 weeks before	8 to 10 weeks before	small	sun	slow
Parsley	up to 6 weeks before	6 to 16 weeks before	small	partial shade	moderate
Parsnip	6 to 8 weeks before	———	small	partial shade	slow
Peas, Garden	2 to 8 weeks before	2 to 12 weeks before	large	sun	moderate
Peas, Black-eye	2 to 10 weeks after	10 to 12 weeks before	large	sun	moderate
Peppers (bedding plants)	1 to 8 weeks after	12 to 16 weeks before	small	sun	moderate
Potatoes	4 to 6 weeks before	14 to 16 weeks before	large	sun	slow

*See figure 1, chapter 1, for freeze dates in Central Texas.　　**Fast, 30 to 60 days; moderate, 60 to 80 days; slow, 80 or more days.

Crop	Planting Dates (in relation to the last [spring] and first [fall] freeze dates)		Space Require-ments	Light Requirements	Maturity Rate
	Spring	Fall			
Potatoes, Sweet	2 to 8 weeks after	——	large	sun	slow
Radishes	6 weeks before to 4 weeks after	up to 8 weeks before	small	partial shade	fast
Rutabaga	6 to 8 weeks before	12 to 16 weeks before	large	sun	fast
Salsify	4 to 6 weeks before	12 to 16 weeks before	small	partial shade	slow
Shallot	2 to 8 weeks before	6 to 10 weeks before	small	sun	slow
Spinach	1 to 8 weeks before	2 to 16 weeks before	small	partial shade	fast
Spinach, New Zealand	2 to 8 weeks after	12 to 16 weeks before	small	partial shade	fast
Squash, Summer	1 to 4 weeks after	12 to 15 weeks before	large	sun	moderate
Squash, Winter	1 to 4 weeks after	12 to 14 weeks before	large	sun	moderate
Tomato (bedding plants)	2 to 8 weeks after	12 to 14 weeks before	small	sun	moderate
Turnip	2 to 6 weeks before	2 to 12 weeks before	small	sun	fast
Watermelon	2 to 6 weeks after	14 to 16 weeks before	large	sun	slow

Fruits

Blackberries. Although blackberries require a fair amount of space, their adaptability to a wide variety of soil and climatic conditions and their low maintenance demands make them desirable home-garden fruits. Blackberries are biennial, which means that they put on vegetative growth the first year and produce fruit the following year. Prune out only the producing canes after the harvest and destroy them to reduce the risk of anthracnose and rosette, common fungal diseases. New canes should be pinched back during the summer to encourage branching. Be sure to fertilize with a complete fertilizer and water well immediately after pruning.

Recommended Varieties for Central Texas
Brazos, Comanche, and three recently developed varieties from Texas A&M University Agricultural Experiment Station —*Brison, Womack,* and *Rosborough.* These three have very upright canes, which do not require trellising.

Grapes. New developments in grape culture have increased this fruit's potential in Texas. Although well-adapted to many climates, successful grapes will depend on the gardener's selection of varieties suitable to her or his region. Do not expect to grow the common supermarket varieties, such as Thompson Seedless or Tokay, but rather be adventuresome and strike out for new tastes.

While grapes like heat and sandy loam, they will not tolerate sitting in wet soil. We caution against overfertilizing, which will result in lush foliage at the expense of fruit production. Because grapes grow only on new growth, severe pruning before the new growing season begins is essential.

Recommended Varieties for Central Texas. Thriving in alkaline, heavy clay soils and under conditions of extreme heat and drought, the *Champanel* produces a large, black grape in large, loose clusters. It is an excellent choice for a grape arbor. Similar in fruit to the Concord, which does not do well here, the *Fredonia* produces large, compact clusters of black grapes. Hardy, vigorous, and disease-resistant, the *Seibel 9110* produces a semi-seedless, medium-sized, yellow grape. It is strongly recommended for north to south Central Texas by the Texas Agricultural Extension Service.

Strawberries. Providing pleasant evergreen foliage as well as delicious fruit, strawberries do demand space, full sun, and good drainage. For urban and smaller suburban gardens, culture in a specially constructed, tiered bed is recommended. Each tier should be filled with two parts coarse sand, one part sphagnum moss, and one part top soil, to a depth of at least ten inches. Before setting out plants, apply 6–12–6 fertilizer in the amount specified by the fertilizer directions. Strawberry plants must not be allowed to dry out; therefore a polyethylene or straw mulch is absolutely necessary.

Recommended Varieties:

North Central Texas: Plant *Blakemore, Dixieland, Pocahontas,* and *Sunrise* in the spring. Fruits will be produced the following spring.

Central Texas: Plants are set out in the fall and the fruit is harvested the following spring. *Fresno, Florida Ninety, Daybreak,* and *Sequoia* are good producers.

West Central Texas: Gem, Ozark Beauty, and *Ogallala* do well here.

Trouble in the Garden

Come forth into the light of things
Let Nature be your teacher.
William Wordsworth,
"The Tables Turned"

If you have had trouble in the garden with disease and insects (and in this climate, who hasn't?), then you know that diagnosing and curing problems is no simple matter. Nonetheless, there is some general information that can be of help, and there are some specific suggestions for handling the most common troublemakers.

Just as with humans, in plants prevention is the best cure for disease. While it is true that we can't always predict what will make a plant healthy, there are certain guidelines that do prove helpful to the gardener. Of first importance is the careful selection of plants. There are vegetables, small fruits, and flowering annual plants that are disease-resistant; check your agricultural extension bulletins and seed packages for this information. There are also some species of trees and shrubs that are resistant to specific diseases; see for example, the list of plants resistant to cotton root rot, page 189.

Generally speaking, native plants do better in terms of health, and perhaps that's why you see so many yaupon hollies and mountain laurels in our gardens. Conversely, there are plants like euonymus that are so prone to mildew and scale they can become a burden; and roses, although their beauty is celebrated, require constant care during the blooming seasons if they are to flourish. So be sure to ask questions when you select plants, and try to pick either species that have some resistance to insects and disease or species in which these troublemakers can be controlled.

Another aspect of trouble prevention is variety. Whether

you're selecting vegetables, fruits, shrubs, trees, or flowers, diversity is the key word for avoiding disease and insect infestation. This is why crop rotation has become so important to the home gardener as well as the commercial grower. A good rule to follow is to avoid growing crops of the same family in the same location season after season, since families tend to have the same diseases (see the table on page 185 for a list of such families). Diversity also helps prevent depletion of soil nutrients, since plants take from and deposit into the soil different ingredients.

You should also consider companion planting. This means choosing plants for their compatibility and the mutual benefits they offer each other. It includes using plants with different root depths near one another so they don't compete for nutrients and staggering the height of plants so they can all get sunshine. Another aspect of companion planting is choice of plants that have features other plants need. For instance, you can use marigolds in a vegetable garden to repel the nematodes in nearby plants,[1] or you can make sure you have annuals that attract bees, which are needed for cross pollination.

Speaking of insects, don't overlook the other beneficial ones besides bees. The small lady beetle or ladybug enjoys meals of soft-bodied insects such as aphids, mealybugs, whiteflies, spider mites, and scales. Watch for ladybugs' yellow to orange eggs, found in clusters on the underside of leaves in the spring. Incidentally, some people "import" beneficial bugs, buying them from seed catalogues, for example; however, on small residential lots these bugs are difficult to contain.

Of course, nature provides other assistants, too, such as birds, which thrive on insects. One example is the purple martin, and gardeners often put up special houses for these helpers to attract them to the landscape.

When you have picked the species, the next step is to be sure you purchase the hardiest members of the group. Even the best gardener needs to have good stock to be successful.

---

[1]According to the *Sunset Guide to Organic Gardening*, marigolds give off chemicals called root diffusates, which can be toxic to nematodes. Test plots with marigolds had as many as ninety percent fewer nematodes than test plots without marigolds.

Table 1

Plant Groups with Diseases in Common

Group A	Group B	Group C
Watermelon	Cabbage	Pepper
Cucumber	Cauliflower	Tomato
Squash	Brussels sprouts	Potato
Cantaloupe	Rutabaga	Eggplant
Honeydew melon	Turnip	Okra
Pumpkin	Mustard	
	Radish	
	Collards	
	Lettuce	
	Swiss chard	
	Spinach	
Group D	**Group E**	**Group F**
Carrots	Sweet corn	Beans
Sweet potatoes	Small grains	Peas
Beets	Coastal bermuda grass	Cowpeas
Onions	Sorghum	
Garlic	Sudan grass	
Shallots		

SOURCE: Jerral D. Johnson. *Disease Prevention in the Home Garden.* MP-954/revised. College Station: Texas Agricultural Extension Service, 1975.

After your plants have been properly selected and planted, adequate care becomes the main concern. Proper feeding, watering, pruning, and weeding are vital to a good growth process. Continual maintenance includes removing old plant material such as leaves, weeds, and dead stems, which invite pests and disease. It is also beneficial to keep the soil broken up and free of a hard surface crust. In the winter this practice may help get rid of any hibernating insects that have burrowed under the top soil; they will probably expire when exposed to the cold.

In chapter 3 we talked about the use of fences to provide

privacy for the homeowner. Fences also help protect the yard from unwanted weeds and animals, such as deer and stray dogs. Some people use short border fences to keep young children and rambunctious pets out of flower beds and gardens. To keep other small animals such as raccoons away, we suggest the use of humane traps. These can be purchased in many hardware stores. The animals that are caught can be released unharmed in areas outside the city, with permission of the landowner.

Another simple preventive measure is washing away potential troublemakers with the hose. Much less popular and much more work is handpicking some of them, such as snails and slugs.

Until now we have concentrated on the prevention of problems from natural causes. But disease and insects aren't the only threats to a healthy environment. Landfill can affect the growth of trees and even threaten their survival. Unfortunately, in areas where construction is prevalent, this is a recurring problem, and the effects may not be obvious for several months or even several years. When fill is placed over the root system of a tree, it may be more difficult for enough water to reach the roots. There is also a reduction in the oxygen supply to roots. The lack of oxygen may cause the accumulation of gases and chemicals detrimental to good growth. When this happens, the feeder roots don't develop, the roots die, and the tree above the ground begins to deteriorate. To remedy the situation, it is necessary to provide aeration through construction of a tree well or by several other methods that are described in bulletin L-1309 from the Texas Agricultural Extension Service. This bulletin is available from your county extension agent.

Furthermore, if the grade is lowered near the tree roots, there can be drought damage resulting from the loss of roots. According to the bulletin: "Terraces or retaining walls can be used to avoid soil loss in the area of greatest root growth. . . . Much of the top growth should be thinned out by trimming out the lateral growth [of the tree] and cutting some of the main branches back to good side branches. In this way the normal growth of the tree is retained while the top growth can be reduced to a third or at least a half of its original size."

In reality, landfill problems, as well as the other troubles mentioned, may not always be preventable. Nonetheless, being aware of them can allow you at least to minimize the damage.

The next stage after prevention is detection. If you have a gardening friend, take regular tours through each other's gardens —four eyes are better than two. Examine the plants carefully. If you find leaves that are chewed, punctured, streaked, or dotted, there are probably insects on the scene. On the other hand, if you find brown, black, or yellow spots or spots with a thin, watery appearance, you're apt to be dealing with disease.

Be sure to check regularly for chlorosis, a common problem in this area. The leaves (and grass too) turn yellow between the veins; eventually entire leaves may appear yellow. To correct this situation, spray or use soil applications of iron sulfate (copperas) or iron chelate. Remember that plants near the foundation of a building are more apt to have this problem, due to seepage from the limestone.

Two other common problems are lack of water and fertilizer burn. To survive our long, hot summer, plants need frequent watering—especially plants like azaleas, which seem to turn brown overnight. If the water supply has been adequate and you find more brown leaves that look burned, you may have used too much fertilizer or applied it improperly.

Premature leaf loss often occurs in late summer if the season has been very hot and dry. Frequently owners mistake this for disease symptoms, when actually the tree is only shedding the luxuriant greenery it can no longer support. No permanent damage is caused, and the tree will leaf out normally next spring.

As anyone who gardens knows, even the best attempts to keep plants healthy can fail. Determining what is wrong and curing the problem are not simple matters. Even nurserymen and plant experts sometimes disagree, and you may not be able to get a prescription in time to save the patient. We have listed below some likely remedies for the most common plant diseases and insects. Keep in mind that in most cases there is more than one product that can be used, and certainly we have not attempted to name them all. We have usually given the common name required in the list of ingredients on the label. In some cases, though, we have used a trade name, which refers to a specific product (these are capitalized).

Due to the growing concern over using pesticides in the environment, we asked the Travis County horticulturist what he thought could be safely recommended as standard items for gardeners. He recommended three fungicides—captan, benomyl, and maneb—and three insecticides—diazinon, Sevin, and Kelthane. Benomyl is a systemic, general-purpose fungicide used for mildew, mold, and so forth. Captan is used for fungus diseases of flowers and ornamentals. Maneb is used for controlling fungus diseases of vegetables and fruit. Of the insecticides, diazinon (Spectracide and other brands) is used for the largest number of insects, including aphids, leaf miners, scale, chinch bugs, cockroaches, ants, crickets, silverfish, spiders, and sowbugs (pillbugs). Sevin is the trade name for carbaryl, which is used on beetles, caterpillars, leaf miners, some scale, and turf insects. Kelthane is used to control mites.

Bordeaux Mixture is recommended for some fungi. It is available in a powder, which is mixed with water, or you can start from scratch. Mix three teaspoons of copper sulphate in three quarts of water in a wooden, earthenware, or glass container. In another, one-gallon container, stir five teaspoons of hydrated lime (60 to 80 percent calcium oxide) into one quart of water. Pour the copper solution into the lime, stirring rapidly. Apply two to three hours after preparing.

We might add that if you choose malathion, listed below, which is used for a number of insects, it is necessary in areas like Austin to add one teaspoon of vinegar to a gallon of water before putting in the malathion. Otherwise the overly alkaline water will deactivate the malathion and make it ineffective.

Fungicides and insecticides are available in wettable powder sprays, liquid concentrates, or dusts, which are applied directly to plants and can't be used as sprays. The liquid sprays are easy to work with, especially if you use a hose sprayer. A small container of the fungicide or insecticide is attached to the hose, and the proper proportion of water dilutes the substance when the water is turned on. If you don't use a hose sprayer, you will have to mix the spray solution with water by hand in a separate container, preferably a gallon-size watering can that is kept on hand for this purpose only.

To do a larger area, you may want to get a small power sprayer from a rental equipment company. There are also large power
dusters (and airplanes, too) available for doing orchards, but most
of us can rely on small hand dusters. Remember that while dust
doesn't need mixing and is easy to apply, it cannot be used in the
wind, and it is sometimes more expensive.

Whatever method and material you choose, be certain to read
and follow the directions on the container. Take other precautions,
too. Keep these materials labeled and stored outside the house,
preferably in a locked cabinet away from children. Avoid inhal-
ing fumes from pesticides, and wear rubber gloves when handling
them. Most important, don't overdo it; use pesticides prudently.
After all is said and done, what's a Texas garden without a supply
of good, healthy bugs?

Common Diseases

Anthracnose. These fungi cause leaf edges of diseased plants
to have V-shaped spots, while spots in the centers may be angular
or circular. Twigs may die back, and cankers may occur on limbs.
Apply Bordeaux Mixture on trees, such as oaks and sycamores,
and maneb on flowers, such as pansies and carnations.

Cankers. These fungi cause black or brown, irregular dead
areas that may encircle stems, branches, or even trunks. This causes
dieback, where the whole top of the tree may appear brown and
dead. It is common in Lombardy poplars, cottonwoods, willows,
and mulberries, as well as in gardenias and roses. Affected shrubs
should be destroyed; to treat trees, cut out the dead areas or limbs.
If trunks are affected, tree surgery may be needed. Disinfect pruning shears after each cut by dipping them in a solution of one part
household bleach to nine parts water. Use a disinfectant sealer on
cuts and wounds.

Cotton Root Rot. This rot is a soil-borne disease that suddenly
kills seemingly healthy plants. It is most likely to occur from June
to September and is usually characterized by rapid death of the
affected plant, although trees may survive a year or so. Leaves on
trees (and other plants) turn yellow because of the deteriorating

root systems, but this is also a symptom of other problems, such as improper watering. Plants are easily removed from the soil and show decayed bark. Unfortunately, no current fungicide has proven effective in controlling the disease. The best prevention is to buy plants that are moderately to highly resistant to the disease. These include: bald cypress, boxwood, cedar elm, crape myrtle, holly, honeysuckle, juniper, live oak, pecan, pyracantha, redbud, red cedar, red oak, and sycamore. The trees and plants that are most susceptible are: apple, chinaberry, Chinese tallow, cottonwood, elm (not cedar elm), fruitless mulberry, ligustrum, loquat, roses, silver maple, and willow.

Damping Off. This root disease affects seedlings or young plants and may cause them to die. The roots and the stems at the soil surface show symptoms of rotting. Root and stem rot (see below) may be a continuation of this seedling blight. In addition to the treatment given for that, check the manufacturer's directions for treating seeds with captan or thiram as a preventive. You may also sterilize small lots of soil before planting by baking the soil in a 160-degree oven for three to four hours.

Fire Blight. Symptoms of fire blight are easily identified: branch tips die back, giving the affected limbs a scorched, burned appearance. The chemical Kocide is effective as a preventive if you spray it when the tree is in full bloom. Once the symptoms appear, pruning out affected branches can help prevent the spread of the disease; spraying the blossoms weekly during the blooming period with Bordeaux Mixture may also help. There is, however, no guaranteed cure. Tools must be cleaned with a chlorine solution between cuts to avoid spreading the disease. Apples, pears, and the rose family are very susceptible to these bacteria, as are cotoneaster, Indian hawthorne, loquat, pyracantha, photinia, and quince.

Leaf Spot (bacterial). Water-soaked spots that turn brown and irregular make leaf spot identifiable because of their ringlike appearance with a "bull's eye" center. Treat with Bordeaux Mixture every two to four weeks. Destroy diseased leaves that drop from the plants. Plants that are susceptible to bacterial leaf spot include: begonia, boxwood, chrysanthemum, delphinium, dogwood, elm, gardenia, gladiolus, iris, maple, narcissus, peony, phlox, privet, and sycamore.

Leaf Spot (fungal). Fungal leaf spot is characterized by growing spots, which may run together and cause leaves to drop. There may be tiny pinpoints in the dead spots. Treat with maneb, captan, folpet, or zineb, applying at seven- to ten-day intervals when the disease first occurs. Destroy dead leaves. Check labels on fungicides for lists of other plants on which use is recommended. We might point out that in roses black spot (a form of leaf spot in which circular black areas appear on the leaf) can usually be prevented by regular applications of fungicides, including benomyl, maneb, and folpet (see roses, chapter 9). Many other plants and trees are susceptible to fungal leaf spot, for example: ashes, carnations, chrysanthemums, cottonwoods, dogwoods, elms, hollyhocks, irises, marigolds, mulberries, pansies, sycamores, and zinnias.

Petal Blight. Azaleas and camellias sometimes get distorted leaf and bud growth with white, thickened areas. Treat with Terraclor by spraying before the buds open and again after they flower.

Powdery Mildew. One of the most common problems in our humid climate, powdery mildew appears as white or gray mold on the leaf bud or twig and causes leaves and flowers to be deformed. It is most apt to attack chrysanthemums, crape myrtle, euonymus, phlox, roses, and zinnias. As soon as you spot the disease, spray with benomyl, Karathane, or Acti-dione PM.

Root and Stem Rot. The foliage of affected plants will turn yellow and appear stunted. Brown or black spots of different shapes and sizes occur on the stem at or near the soil surface and on roots. The tips of small roots decay, and eventually there is complete rotting of the roots. Treat with PCNB (pentachloronitrobenzene, marketed under the brand name Terraclor) or zineb. Avoid overwatering or crowding plants.

Rust. Several fungi cause rust to appear sometimes on plants. Orange, rusty red, brown, or black raised spots occur on the underside of leaves. They can be rubbed off and are easily identified on a white cloth. Use zineb or maneb at seven- to fourteen-day intervals. Pick and destroy diseased leaves. On twigs, branches, or galls (swelling on stems and branches), rust appears as orange or red swellings. Cut and destroy galls; prune and destroy infected limbs during the winter.

Insects

In addition to the specific remedies listed below, there are available systemic insecticides of a more general nature, which can

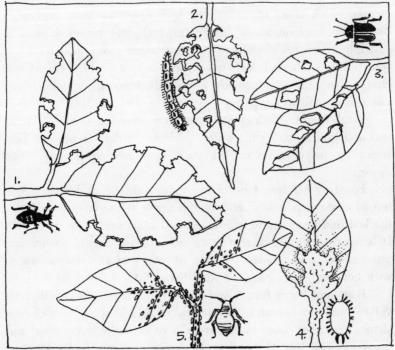

INSECTS: 1. WEEVILS 2. CATERPILLARS 3. BEETLES 4. SPIDER MITES 5. APHIDS

be used for a variety of different plants. Systemic insecticides have chemicals that, when absorbed by the plant, keep insects away.

Red Spider Mites. Fine webs on plants tell you that spider mites are at work. You can see these small invaders on the undersides of leaves of practically any kind of plant. Use Kelthane to control.

Scale. Masses of green, brown, or purple dots, usually found on the underside of leaves but sometimes on stems and fruits, indicate the presence of scale. These insects have protective shells; they suck the juices of a plant and destroy it. Common host plants are camellia and hibiscus, both of which have scale that is white, and gardenia, jasmine, and schefflera. To control, spray with a garden-type oil emulsion in the spring or fall, when the temperature is below eighty-five degrees and above forty-five degrees for at least a week.

Sowbugs, also called **Pillbugs.** These dark gray, fat, hard-shelled bugs are rampant invaders of vegetable gardens, flower beds, and sometimes garages. When disturbed, they roll up into a ball. Preferring dark, moist places, they can be discouraged by the removal of garden debris. Apply diazinon or malathion in areas where they collect.

Nematodes. Leaf and root nematodes are microscopic worms; some kinds that grow in hot dry soil are called root-knot nematodes. Most ornamentals are susceptible, especially boxwood, fig, gardenia, and passionflower, as well as chrysanthemums, and other annuals. In the vegetable garden tomatoes and okra are major victims. Affected plants lose color, appear stunted, and may gradually die. Diseased plants have swollen and irregular roots, or brown or black spots or streaks on the roots. Because many nemacides also kill all other insects, earthworms, and plants, be sure to read the manufacturer's instructions before applying the chemical.

Aphids. These small white, greenish-white, or red and black insects puncture leaves, creating openings for a virus. The new leaves of a pecan tree may be curled, pansies deformed, and sooty mold seen on crape myrtle. Aphids can be controlled with malathion, Sevin, or diazinon.

Caterpillars, Snails, Slugs, Beetles, and Earwigs. These are probably the villains when blossoms are badly chewed. Use diazinon or bug bait for snails and slugs, diazinon or Sevin for beetles and earwigs.

Tent Caterpillars. They can engulf entire limbs in massive webs. Since penetration of the web is necessary for chemical control, pruning out the affected areas is often most effective. Although tent caterpillars infest a variety of hosts, the pecan and the mulberry are particularly susceptible. To treat, add a quarter-teaspoon of ammonia to a gallon of an oil-based spray.

Thrips. These tiny, winged, sucking insects cause streaked foliage, only partial opening of flowers, or brown edges on petals. They are difficult to control and are best prevented by spraying with malathion. Another reason for "balled" flowers is a sudden drop in humidity, which causes moisture problems; this can be prevented by keeping the plant well watered.

Mealybugs. White, cottony webs appear on leaves and stems when mealybugs are present. The plants are weakened and will die if they are not treated. These pests attack many ornamentals, including azaleas and coleus. Use cotton dipped in alcohol to remove the bugs. Then treat with malathion.

Gardening Calendar for Central Texas

Shed no tear—O shed no tear!
The flowers will bloom another year.
John Keats, "Faery Songs, I"

How fortunate that our climate makes it a pleasure to be a year-round gardener. As with many hobbies, preparation and planning increase the dividends. The following calendar will, we hope, serve as a guide in organizing monthly tasks and projects.

January

1. Plan your garden by gathering ideas and preparing a sketch of what goes where.
2. Plant bare-root roses, fruit trees, and landscape plants. Container-grown roses may be planted whenever available, but if possible avoid hottest summer months.
3. Remove fall garden debris and keep the lawn free from dead leaves. Pick up camellia blossoms from the ground to help prevent camellia petal blight.
4. Prepare gardens for spring and summer annuals by tilling the soil and adding peat moss or compost. Fertilize fruit trees. Avoid working wet soil.
5. Begin to "harden" cabbage or broccoli plants in cold frames by less watering and some exposure to cold. Do not over-harden, or plants will be woody.
6. If necessary, spray dormant oil to control scale on fruit and landscape trees on days when the temperatures will be above forty degrees for twelve hours.

7. Begin seeding pepper and tomato plants in cold frames for early transplants. Sow annual and perennial flower seeds in cold frames.

8. Apply preemergent weed killer to lawns. Read and follow instructions on labels.

9. Be sure to water trees, shrubs, and lawns during dry periods.

10. Collect hardwood cuttings to be used for budding and grafting in April.

11. Plant recommended blackberry varieties: Brazos, Comanche, TAMU Brison, Rosborough, and Womack.

February

1. Continue planting deciduous and evergreen trees and shrubs. Plant bare-root roses until the middle of the month.

2. Aphids begin to appear on ornamentals and should be controlled with malathion, Sevin, or diazinon.

3. Plant cool-season vegetables (see chapter 12). Transplant previously seeded broccoli and cabbage.

4. Begin spraying program for fruit trees; check with your county extension agent.

5. Prune fruit and nut trees, landscape trees, evergreens, summer-flowering shrubs, and roses (not climbing roses).

6. Plant disease-free Irish seed potatoes. Bed sweet potatoes in cold frames.

7. Treat ash and sycamore trees with Thuricide for tent caterpillars and maneb or Bordeaux Mixture for anthracnose.

8. Divide and replant daisies.

9. Begin to harden tomatoes, peppers, etc., in cold frames by less watering and by exposure to cold. Do not overharden.

10. Pear varieties such as Orient, Kieffer, or Maxine planted now will produce delicious fruit later. Follow recommended spray schedules.

11. Irrigate fall-planted strawberries and established blackberries during periods of low rainfall.

March

1. Complete all dormant pruning of evergreens and summer-flowering shrubs in early March.
2. Don't plant fruit and nut trees or any bare-root plants after the first part of March. Balled and burlapped plants may be planted throughout the summer.
3. Fertilize all landscape plants and trees; they need nourishment after the winter.
4. After the last frost (see figure 1), set out annuals such as ageratum, dianthus, morning glory, petunia, phlox, portulaca, and zinnia.
5. Begin planting hardy vegetables such as cucumbers, lettuce, eggplants, etc. (see planting charts, chapter 12).
6. Begin to seed bermuda grass and sod Floratam or other strains of St. Augustine.
7. Turn compost pile and add additional organic matter and a small amount of complete fertilizer.
8. Start some hanging baskets to add to those you've kept inside during the winter. Some popular candidates are petunias, geraniums, and begonias.
9. Prevent black spot on roses by spraying with appropriate fungicide such as benomyl, maneb, or folpet.

April

1. Bed ageratum, amaranthus, copper plants, geranium, periwinkle, portulaca, daisies, and day lilies.
2. Prepare beds and plant annuals such as balsam, cosmos, marigold, periwinkle, petunia, and zinnia.
3. Plant green beans. Set out sweet and hot pepper plants and eggplants.
4. As they finish blooming, fertilize azaleas with azalea fertilizer such as 8-12-4.
5. Begin harvesting beets, broccoli, cabbage, carrots, lettuce, etc. Apply small amount of fertilizer around leafy plants after first harvest, but do not allow fertilizer to touch leaves.
6. Select caladium bulbs and keep them warm and dry until ready to plant at the end of the month. Wait until May to plant in the Dallas–Fort Worth area. Caladiums require warm days and warm nights.
7. Plant okra, sweet potatoes, and Southern peas. Apply mulch around tomatoes, peppers, and eggplants.
8. Prune spring-flowering shrubs after blooming: climbing roses, forsythia, quince, and Indian hawthorne.
9. Seed bermuda grass and keep moist.
10. Check plants for insects. Use malathion on sucking type insects such as aphids and thrips, Kelthane on red spider, and Sevin on chewing insects and worms.
11. Use fungicide such as benomyl to control mildew on roses and vegetable plants.
12. It is natural for some old leaves on certain plants to turn yellow and fall at this time of year, so don't worry if this happens to your magnolia, gardenia, photinia, abelia, ligustrum, and pittosporum.
13. Remove old blackberry canes and pinch back new canes to encourage branching. Water and fertilize throughout the summer.

May

1. Sow amaranthus, balsam, and coleus seeds.
2. Look for chinch bugs later this month and if necessary treat with diazinon.
3. Plant bedding plants of coleus, cockscomb, copper plant, marigold, periwinkle, portulaca, and zinnia.
4. Spray or dust roses with recommended fungicide (Benlate or Phaltan) for black spot. Use insecticide such as malathion or Orthane to control insects. Repeat weekly throughout spring.
5. Check vegetables, especially tomatoes, for spider mites on underside of leaves and use Kelthane to control insects.
6. Use a high-nitrogen fertilizer on your lawn (see chapter 5).
7. Begin to harvest brussels sprouts, onions, potatoes, snap beans, cucumbers, lettuce, squash, blackberries, and peaches.
8. Do not remove the foliage of spring-flowering bulbs until the foliage dies down.
9. Apply small amounts of fertilizer around producing vegetables such as beans, cucumbers, and squash.
10. Caladium bulbs can continue to be planted.
11. Complete pruning of climbing roses.
12. Complete strawberry harvest and remove plants.
13. Dig up ranunculus bulbs. First dry them, then store in an old nylon stocking in a cool place until replanting time next winter.

June

1. Plant bedding plants of amaranthus, ageratum, celosia, coleus, marigold, periwinkle, portulaca, salvia, and zinnia this month and July.

2. Water lawn and garden thoroughly when needed. Give special attention to plants like azaleas and camellias, which are easily damaged by hot, dry weather. Don't forget to water and feed hanging baskets.

3. Pinch back chrysanthemums to encourage branching. Remove gladiolus bulbs after leaves turn brown, and store in a dry place.

4. Harvest lima beans, eggplants, tomatoes, green beans, sweet corn, potatoes, and watermelons.

5. Fertilize annual blooming plants with a balanced fertilizer to assure continued bloom and vigor.

6. Check lawns for grubworms through July. Use diazinon to control.

7. Turn compost pile and moisten.

8. Continue to pinch tips of blackberry bushes to encourage branching. This year's growth will produce next year's berries. Add iron chelate or sulfate to the soil to correct yellowing foliage.

9. Pinch back annuals such as petunias if they become tall and leggy. Then fertilize and water them to encourage growth.

10. Watch for powdery mildew on crape myrtle, zinnias, photinias, and euonymus. Use benomyl or Acti-dione PM to control.

11. Apply mulch such as peat moss or wood chips to flower beds to conserve moisture, lower soil temperature, and reduce weeding.

July

1. Now's the time to think about your fall garden and prepare an area for it. Till, fertilize, and if necessary treat for nematodes (see chapter 13).
2. Plant the same flowering plants recommended for June.
3. Make first seeding of fall eggplants, peppers, okra, and tomatoes.
4. If you're going on vacation for more than four or five days, arrange for someone to attend to your lawn and garden. Water throughly every five to seven days if there is no rain. Some areas may require more frequent watering than others; newly sown plants need special attention.
5. Make final cutting of blackberry canes to promote secondary shoot growth.
6. Divide spring-blooming perennials, including daffodils, day lilies, and irises and replant the best specimens, discarding diseased plants.
7. Fill in low areas of the lawn and garden with small applications of good topsoil.
8. Apply fertilizer to lawn and then water thoroughly (see chapter 5).
9. Check azaleas and camellias for iron chlorosis; the leaves will be yellow-green with dark green veins. If this condition appears, use copperas or iron chelate to correct.
10. By the middle of the month make the last pinch on early-blooming mums. Those that bloom late in the fall can be given one more pinch the last of the month. Be sure to keep them watered.

August

1. Be sure to water frequently and thoroughly during the intense heat. Don't forget the young vegetable plants.
2. This is the end of the lawn-planting season, so make haste with your seed or sprigs and complete the job by September.
3. Plant your fall vegetable garden—green beans, broccoli, cucumbers, lima beans, and carrots.
4. Prepare a planting area for strawberries by lowering the soil pH with a sulphur product and adding quantities of sand and organic matter.
5. Plant for fall and winter gardens: alyssum, cornflower, calendula, candytuft, delphinium, hollyhock, larkspur, petunia, and stock.
6. Prepare to collect leaves as they fall for mulching and for a new compost pile. Water compost pile to aid decomposition.
7. Control weeds in gardens and flower beds.
8. Bluebonnet seeds can be planted now.

September

1. Continue sowing flower seeds listed for August.
2. Begin to harvest sweet potatoes.
3. Check the chart in chapter 12, and continue planting fall vegetables.
4. Apply small amounts of fertilizer around blooming tomatoes, peppers, and eggplants.
5. Plant strawberries of recommended varieties such as Sequoia, Florida Ninety, Daybreak, and Fresno.
6. Divide and plant cannas, day lilies, bearded irises, shasta daisies, and violets.
7. Brown patch is apt to appear on St. Augustine lawns; apply Terraclor or Fore to spots where brown patch is apt to appear or when it first appears in a new location.
8. Fertilize lawns during the September–October period with a low-nitrogen fertilizer (see chapter 5).

October

1. For winter color in the garden try started plants of pansies, snapdragons, and dianthus.
2. Plant container-grown landscape shrubs; they will have a growth advantage when spring arrives.
3. Plant peonies (in the northern part of our region), crocuses and amaryllis.
4. Make additional plantings of parsley, radishes, spinach, greens, and carrots.
5. Annuals that can be sown now include cornflower, larkspur, phlox, poppies, and snapdragons.
6. Select quality tulip bulbs and chill in vegetable tray of refrigerator four to six weeks before planting.
7. Dig and store caladium tubers in dry peat or perlite in an area where the temperature will stay above sixty degrees.
8. Plant bermuda onion seeds for big, sweet bulbs next spring. Make first planting of English peas.
9. Begin new compost pile with fall leaves, or add to the one you have.

November

1. Plant spring-flowering bulbs such as daffodils, crocuses, Dutch irises, ranunculuses, and anemones. Plant tulips after the middle of the month.
2. Fertilize shade trees now for maximum spring growth. Deep root placement in holes is more effective than surface fertilizing.
3. Harvest mature green tomatoes before the first frost. Store at room temperature until red and ripe.
4. Prepare beds for roses to be planted in December and January.
5. Clean flower beds and rework to prepare them for spring planting.
6. Remove debris from flower beds and gardens to control diseases and insects.

December

1. Begin planting bare-root roses, and try some new varieties (see chapter 9.)
2. Although our climate is not ideal for tulips, if you have chilled the bulbs in the refrigerator, now is the time to plant them.
3. Seed California poppies, nasturtiums, and sweet peas.
4. Use dormant oil spray to control scale on camellias, hollies, and euonymus.
5. Begin seeding broccoli, cabbage, lettuce, and impatiens in cold frames for later transplants.
6. Fertilize pansies and spring-flowering perennials with a 5-10-5 fertilizer.
7. Select and plant pecan trees. See chapter 8 for varieties.
8. If ordering seeds for spring annuals, do it now.

Bibliography

Bailey, Leo L. *Step to Step Guide to Landscape and Garden.* Hicksville, N.Y.: Exposition Press, 1974.

Climate of the States. Washington, D.C.: U.S. Government Printing Office, 1969.

A Climatological Summary of Austin, Texas, During the Past 50 Years. Prepared by Weather Modification and Development Division, Texas Water Development Board. Austin, 1976.

Cole, Deborah. *Gardening in Austin and Central Texas.* Austin: Austin Area Gardening Council, 1978.

Conway, H. McKinley, and Linda Liston, eds. *The Weather Handbook.* Atlanta: Conway Research, 1974.

Correll, Donovan S., and Marshall C. Johnston. *Manual of the Vascular Plants of Texas.* Renner, Tex.: Texas Research Foundation, 1970.

Cotner, Sam, and John Larsen. *Home Gardening in Texas.* B-1139/revised. College Station: Texas Agricultural Extension Service, 1977.

Crockett, James. *Annuals: The Time-Life Encyclopedia of Gardening.* New York: Time-Life Books, 1972.

———. *Perennials: The Time-Life Encyclopedia of Gardening.* New York: Time-Life Books, 1977.

Dallas Garden Club of the Dallas Woman's Club. *Dallas Planting Manual for Gardens within 100 Mile Radius.* Dallas, 1970.

Doolittle, Rosalie. *Southwest Gardening.* Albuquerque: University of New Mexico Press, 1967.

Duble, Richard L. *Lawn Care.* L-1372. College Station: Texas Agricultural Extension Service, 1975.

Fisher, Ted. *Ornamental Shrubs for Central and South Texas.* MP-966. College Station: Texas Agricultural Extension Service, 1978.

———. *Shrubs, Vines, and Trees for the Austin Area.* Austin: Travis County Extension Service, 1974.

———, and Gene Sears. *Suggested Planting Dates and Varieties of Vegetables for Travis County.* Austin: Travis County Extension Service, n.d.

Flemer, William, III. *Nature's Guide to Successful Gardening and Landscaping.* New York: Thomas Y. Crowell Co., 1972.

Forest Trees of Texas, How to Know Them. Bullettin 20. College Station: Texas Forest Service, 1971.

Garrett, Howard. *Plants of the Metroplex.* Lantana, 1975.

Gould, F. W. *Texas Plants: A Checklist and Ecological Summary.* MP-585. College Station: Texas Agricultural Experiment Station, 1975.

Growing Ground Covers. Home and Garden Bulletin No. 175. Washington, D.C.: U.S. Department of Agriculture, 1975.

Horne, C. Wendell. *What You Should Know About Plant Diseases.* B-995. College Station: Texas Agricultural Extension Service, 1975.

————, Jerral Johnson, and Walter J. Walls. *Controlling Diseases on Ornamental Plants.* MP-1246. College Station: Texas Agricultural Extension Service, 1976.

Hudson, Charles J., Jr. *Hudson's Southern Gardening.* New York: David McKay Company, 1958.

Hudson, Roy L. *Sunset Pruning Handbook.* Menlo Park, Calif.: Lane Books, 1971.

Hume, Harold. *Gardening in the Lower South.* New York: Macmillan Co., 1954.

Johnson, Jerral D. *Disease Prevention in the Home Garden.* MP-954/revised. College Station: Texas Agricultural Extension Service, 1975.

Kutac, Edward A., and Christopher Caran. *A Bird Finding and Naturalist's Guide for the Austin, Texas, Area.* Austin: Oasis Press, 1976.

Loewer, Peter H. *Seeds and Cuttings.* New York: Walker and Co., 1975.

McEachern, George Ray, and Blueford G. Handcock. *Texas Strawberries.* B-1124. College Station: Texas Agricultural Extension Service, 1976.

Mason, Hamilton. *Your Garden in the South.* New York: D. Van Nostrand Co., 1961.

Nehrling, Arno, and Irene Nehrling. *The Picture Book of Perennials.* New York: Hearthside Press, 1964.

Poincelot, Raymond P. *The Biochemistry and Metholodogy of Composting.* Bulletin 727. New Haven, Connecticut Agricultural Experiment Station, 1972.

Protecting Shade Trees During Home Construction. Home and Garden Bulletin No. 104. Washington, D.C.: U.S. Department of Agriculture, 1975.

Renton, P. A., Jr., H. R. Newcomer, and Roy C. Bates. *Gardening in South Texas.* San Antonio: Naylor Company, 1971.

Rickett, Harold William. *Wild Flowers of the United States: Volume 3, Texas.* New York: McGraw-Hill, 1970.

Ruffner, James A., and Frank E. Blair, eds. *Weather Almanac*. Detroit: Gayle Research, 1977.

Sears, Gene, and Ted Fisher. *Fruit and Nut Varieties for Travis County*. College Station: Texas Agricultural Extension Service, 1976.

Smith, Leon R. *Blackberry Diseases and their Control*. MP-1332. College Station: Texas Agrictultural Extension Service, 1977.

Smith, W. G. *Gardening for Food*. New York: Charles Scribner's Sons, 1972.

Sperry, Neil. *Annual Flowers in the Home Landscape*. College Station: Texas Agricultural Extension Service, 1975.

Sunset Editors. *How to Grow Bulbs*. 3d ed. Menlo Park, Calif.: Lane Books, 1973.

———. *Sunset Guide to Organic Gardening*. Menlo Park, Calif.: Lane Books, 1971.

———. *Sunset Western Garden Book*. Menlo Park, Calif.: Lane Books, 1974.

———. *Vegetable Gardening*. Menlo Park, Calif.: Lane Books, 1971.

TAMU Brison, Rosborough, and Womack, New Blackberry Varieties. L-1528. College Station: Texas Agricultural Experiment Station, 1977.

Taylor, Norman. *Taylor's Encyclopedia of Gardening*. Boston: Houghton Mifflin, 1961.

Trees for Shade and Beauty: Their Selection and Care. Home and Garden Bulletin No. 117. Washington, D.C.: U.S. Department of Agriculture, 1973.

Trees Recommended for North Central Texas. College Station: Texas Agricultural Extension Service, n.d.

U.S. Department of Agriculture, Soil Conservation Service, *Soil Survey of Travis County, Texas*. Washington, D.C.: Government Printing Office, 1975.

Vegetable Varieties for Dallas County and Days to First Harvest. College Station: Texas Agrictural Extension Service, n.d.

Vines, Robert A. *Trees, Shrubs, and Woody Vines of the Southwest*. Austin: University of Texas Press, 1960.

Welch, William C. *Trees for Texas Landscapes*. MP-1151. College Station: Texas Agricultural Extension Service, 1975.

Wyman, Donald. *Wyman's Gardening Encyclopedia*. New York: Macmillan, 1971.

Index

In this index, botanical or scientific names of plants are in *italics*; cross references are made from the scientific name to the most common name. Individual fruit and vegetable varieties and rose varieties are not included. Chemical brand names are not included. A page number in **bold-face** type indicates an illustration.

abelia, 63, 90, **91**, 201
Abelia grandiflora. See abelia
Acacia farnesiana. See huisache
Acalypha wilkesiana. See copper plant
Acer negundo. See boxelder
Acer saccharinum. See silver maple
acidity of soil, 13, 15–16; for roses, 118; for shrubs, 92, 95, 99; for trees, 70
Adiantum pedatum. See maidenhair fern
aeration (of soil), 13, 20, 22, 42
agarita, 90
Agave americana. See century plant
ageratum, 135, 200, 201, 203
Ageratum spp. *See* ageratum
Ailanthus altissima. See tree-of-heaven
ajuga, 48, 49, **49**
Ajuga reptans. See ajuga
Albizia julisbrissin. See mimosa
aleppo pine, 65
Algerian ivy, 125
alkalinity of soil, 15–16, 17, 92, 99, 103
Allium schoenoprasum. See chives
aloe yucca, 115
Althaea rosea. See hollyhock
althea. *See* shrub althea
alyssum, 135, 205
amaranthus, 135, 201, 202, 203
amaryllis, 157, 207

Amaryllis belladonna. See amaryllis
American beautyberry, 91
American elm, 65
Ampelopsis arborea. See peppervine
anemone, 4, **155**, 157, 208
Anemone coronaria. See anemone
annuals, 5, 130, 132–134, **132**, 186, 195, 197–198, 203, 209; diseases of, 185; fertilizer for, 131, 133, 134; planting of, 133, 200, 201, 207; transplanting of, 133; watering of, 133–134
anthracnose, 191, 199
Antigonon leptopus. See mountain rose coralvine
Antirrhinum spp. *See* snapdragon
ants, 190
aphids, 186, 190, **194**, 195, 199, 201
apple tree, 85, 86, 192
aralia, 91
Aralia sieboldii. See aralia
Arborvitae. *See* Chinese arborvitae
Arbutus texana. See Texas madrone
Arizona ash, 65–66, 193, 199
Arizona cypress, 66
Asiatic jasmine, 126, **126**; as ground cover, 121. *See also* jasmine
asparagus, 169, 175, 180; light requirements of, 9
asparagus fern, 45, 49–50
Asparagus sprengeri. See asparagus fern